SURFING INTO PARADISE

Relating Heaven's amazing rescue and recovery operation for the Indian Ocean Tsunami victims, alongside enormous human endeavour on Earth

Channelled by
SIGRID KRISTY

CHANNELLED LIGHT PRESS

(This is a non-profit making book seeking to collect further relief funds for all major disasters past, present and future)

SURFING INTO PARADISE

First Edition October 2006
ISBN No: 0-955306-0-8 / 978-0-95534906-0-4

British Library Cataloguing-in-Publication Data
A record of this book will be available from the British Library

Cover design by MALCOLM DUFFITT

Cover photograph by kind permission of KUONI TRAVEL LTD
(The Anatara Royal Cocoa Palm Resort and Spa, Thailand)

Published by:

CHANNELLED LIGHT PRESS
PO Box 143, Edenbridge, TN8 9AR
info@channelledlightpress.co.uk
www.channelledlightpress.co.uk

Dedicated

- to the thousands of victims caught in the Tsunami catastrophe;
- to the thousands of relatives mourning their dead;
- to the thousands of volunteers, emergency services and aid converging upon the devastated Indian Ocean Zones badly hit by this natural disaster;
- to the heavenly contingencies, who brought their unseen rescues, comfort and compassion to bear upon the new spirit souls, and the aftermath on Earth; and finally,
- to the spirit communicators of this documentary, who seek to bring this moving sequel to the world.

May peace and love be with you all.

Forward

Imagine life without pain. Imagine a society where all act only from love and the highest altruistic motives. Imagine a world where tensions, resentment and envy have no place.

Prepare yourself gently, for, on reading these pages, you are going to enter such a world, the world the Tsunami victims entered, and you can only benefit from this story by being open to the best in yourself and all others.

Be open too, as the author says, to the idea that God does not cause or condone disasters such as the Tsunami. God is the eternal witness to man's actions. All our human behaviour has an inevitable resound and reaction. The result of our thoughtless and massive pillaging of the planet for selfish gain and profit upsets the natural order, and the ensuing turmoil is manifested in natural disasters.

The author is to be thanked for her dedication to her beautiful task. It is bound to bring surprises and joy to the bereaved, and is likely to fascinate and uplift many others.

Kindly contributed by **PEG HOLDEN-PETERS**

Acknowledgements

My grateful thanks and appreciation to the following people:-

CHRISSIE DENHAM — who typed out the entire manuscript from the original writings.

CAROL WILLIAMS — who carried out the proof reading and editing.

MALCOLM DUFFITT — for the beautiful book cover design, advertising media, logo and setting up our world wide web.

KUONI TRAVEL LTD — for granting us their kind permission to use the stunning beach scene of the Anatara Royal Cocoa Palm Resort and Spa, Thailand, for our front cover.

ALISON WHITE — for giving us kind permission to print her channelled contribution © 'Shine Brightly, Children of Light'.

CY COMBES — for kindly passing on 'A Blessing of the Birds' (Author unknown).

DESIGN TO PRINT — who carried out the first printed and bound edition for Channelled Light Press.

PETER CROWSLEY — promotion and co-ordinating assistant.

CHRISTINE HEATH — marketing and sales assistant.

STEPHANIE THOMAS — of 'Buss Murton' solicitors for providing appropriate contracts, and lodging the copyright under safe keeping.

CLOSE FAMILY AND FRIENDS — for their loving support throughout the entire process.

Contents

Brief Preface

2nd January 2005 7.22pm

After watching the TV programme, 'Seven Days that Shook the World', my close friend and I sat in five minutes silence...In those moments of stillness I felt strongly inspired to take up my pen and begin the 'sequel of survival' from the 'other side' of life, through spirit communication by the means of clairaudient dictation taken down in writing, an unexpected gift, which I have had the privilege to develop over the past twenty-four and a half years. During that period I have transcribed many lovely descriptions from the Spirit dimensions, received words of higher wisdom and knowledge, taken down personal communications from individuals, but above all, have taken down considerable information on various major disasters, from short documentaries to whole books, all of which are designed to bring comfort and hope for the bereaved.

Normally I am not motivated to write a disaster testimony for weeks or months after the terrible event. But in this case, quite unexpectedly, I felt compelled to find pen and paper, turn off the phone, have a little to eat to boost my energies, place a glass of water beside me, and settle myself on the sofa to write. The time was *now*!

About thirty-six hours earlier, the previous day, I had been preparing breakfast. My thoughts were reflecting upon the very recent Tsunami disaster, when I received a very brief inspiring vision of spirit rescuers from Heaven surfing through the waves to lift up the 'out-of-body' souls of those drowning in the horrific waves, and carry them gently into the next dimension. It was very moving, but also very uplifting. The first glimmer of this sequel from the 'other side' was coming through.

I knew I was to take down the descriptions at some point over the year. I was still working on a previous story. But tonight I realised this one was more urgent. I must begin straight away! So I will offer my comments and explain my background and psychic life story at the end. The title that came into my mind for this documentary was:- "SURFING INTO PARADISE". I will waste no more time. The dates and times from now on will be the Spirit communications.

May the deepest peace, love, strength and comfort be with all the victims, all the injured, all the bereaved, all the rescuers on Earth, all the international help and aid, and above all, with all the stricken nations and islands tragically caught in this apocalyptic catastrophe, and facing complete demolition of their homes, health and livelihoods. My own heart reaches out to them all very deeply.

I now prepare myself in meditation not having any idea of who will communicate this story, or how it will unfold...

(Note:- May I suggest you read only one Part at a time with a long interval in between. For those of you who are unused to Spirit communications, the new concepts may be a little overwhelming; and for those of you who have tragically lost loved ones in this terrible catastrophe it may awaken strong emotions , which I hope will become calm and serene by the end of the story. Also, the heavenly words may carry healing light vibrations, and too much reading at one time may make you peacefully drowsy.)

Part One

SURFING TO THE RESCUE

2nd January 2005 7.52pm

"I'm an ex-Australian surfer from Bondi Beach. Can you hear me clearly?"

"Yes I can, this is quite a surprise! Thank you so much for coming through."

"It's my privilege to begin this story from our side of life in Heaven. Others will take up their parts as we move through the whole documentary, which has been collated very quickly for you and the world's benefit. Like your special TV programme, the aftermath in these Realms is still being sifted through stage by stage.

But I must state here that our 'time' is considerably faster than yours. We do not have time as you know it, but we do in our own sense. We can make our 'time' go forwards and backwards with thought, which is the basis of our existence. Thought, mental and emotional creates our surroundings, our activities, our visions, our ambitions, our work and spiritual development. In this horrendous disaster you have suffered on Earth, our thought wavelengths have been magnified to help us help you in these devastating circumstances.

We knew long before your Christmas that this super earthquake was to take place. But how do you warn a world, which is in the main ignorant of our existence? Many of you believe in an afterlife in a vague way, that you will go to Heaven and perhaps meet loved ones gone long before you, and maybe meet Jesus, or any other religious figurehead. But how many of you, if any, are aware of our amazing rescue services? Brothers and sisters on Earth you do not stand alone in these times of devastation. We are with you every step of the way, before, during, and after the terrible events, which tear your minds and hearts apart. I was no different to you.

My attitude in physical life was that if there was something of life beyond death, show me! Well nobody did! So I came here totally unprepared for a new existence, because I didn't take any time to look into it on Earth. I thought I knew it all, and found I knew nothing, and felt pretty silly as I got to know how ignorant I had been.

When the alarm bells rang out loud and clear in our Realms of this pending earthquake below the sea, and the call for experienced surfers went out, I enlisted straight away. It was my personal opportunity to thank God for keeping me safe and happy in lower Heaven, and to do something for the cause, which was likely to be the biggest catastrophe in modern times. I wanted to be in on the scene and help others into the Heaven I had come to know. When I was approached to give this communication contribution and take part in this special documentary for Earth, I was completely taken aback, but very honoured.

I know many of you will want to throw the likelihood of this being true and sincere out of the window, whilst others will take it on board and want to know more about our life after death. You're going to come here anyway one day!

The poor victims of this appalling natural tragedy have arrived here far sooner than they expected! None of us know the day or hour when it will be our turn. Bear that in mind. If you can begin to accept now, it may be easier for you when the time comes to settle down into your new 'life'. For those caught totally unaware as the huge waves crashed onto the beaches in the Indian Ocean Zone, there is now quite a period ahead of accepting the truth of their loss of life thrust upon them 'out of the blue', and the shock and confusion of the sudden happening. But this part will be narrated by others. For the moment please know they are safe and 'alive' in our lower Heaven called the 'Summerlands'. More later on that subject.

Let me begin my story now following my enlisting as a member of the surfing teams, which ran into thousands! When we assembled at the auditorium to be given this initial talk of instructions, it was like standing in the crowded stands of a football match, and our auditorium pitch was one of several! It blew my mind completely as we watched a film on a large screen, that we had in front of us, about the rescue operation! You might interrupt me here and say, "What's the need of rescuing souls anyway, they will automatically go to Heaven." Well they do, but let's just say they need a little guiding hand to help it go really smoothly.

So here I was with some thousands of other volunteers watching the horror film before us! No detail was left out, I can tell you. This was to test just how much we were prepared to do the task, and if we wanted to pull out now, well this was the time to speak up. I had to admit I was in two minds, like everyone else who confessed later, but something held us in like a wave of radiance surrounding us, and when that strength ebbed away no-one flinched a muscle. It was as if God held us all in His loving power and He would look after us to look after others. It was as simple as that. Not one solitary soul who had volunteered their services walked out. How could you?

5.1.05 - 8.45pm

Well that was just the beginning! Personal interrogations came next, talking to an experienced rescue officer, who probed into every nook and cranny of your soul, testing your reactions to the various likely reverberations of the operation ahead. By the time you came out of these sessions you felt like you had been verbally pummelled to the ground. But I'm glad now, because when the reality came I felt more confident of my true motives and actions. All the same, *nothing* really prepared us for the enormity of the task.

Next came the practice runs at sea surfing the biggest waves I had ever seen! The organisers purposefully set up a storm to make it really choppy. We were taken out in large boats a little way from the shore and turned out onto the ocean, a hundred at a time to surf back to the beach.

I shall never forget that first time. As we were lowered into the water, surfboard in readiness, to catch the next wave as it thrust the boat on top, we took our cue and began to ride its crest towards land. A hundred others were doing the same desperately keeping their balance like myself. Our previous land drill had taught us to hold ourselves proud in thought to create a stable mind and concentration. It worked! The exhilaration was fantastic! Amazingly, we all made it onto the sand and collapsed in relief. Over the weeks we were taken farther and farther out to sea to ride the waves back to shore, but they kept getting bigger!

The next stage was to actually ride through the waves, and some were up to nearly 50 feet high! Boy, did I sweat over that first practice run. I was so scared I just couldn't think at all! My legs went to pulp, my arms hung helplessly by my side, my stomach turned over, and my head just swam round and round! Luckily an instructor was right behind me, surfed alongside me, and we went through together. Boy oh boy! What an experience! We came out the other side to feel yet another large swell taking us up and up, as if we were mounting the 'Everest' of all waves! The view ahead was amazing. We rode the crest before it rolled over towards the shore ahead, where hundreds of dummy bodies were lying on the beach acting out the scene as it would be on the dreaded day!

This was the real test! We were to grab the snorkels strapped around our waist, slip them over our noses, and dive into the foaming water as it began to crash onto the sand, and reach out for the nearest 'body' floating up to the surface.

A huge fleet of white water rafts followed behind for us to deposit each body before going back to collect another, and so on. Speed was of the essence. A hundred of us gathered every make-believe body from the flooded shore. As the last one was safely laid on a raft, the scene changed miraculously, like a movie film, and we found ourselves riding the dozens of life saving rafts over gentle waves onto another calm and very beautiful beach, where the rescued 'bodies' were laid quietly under the palm trees to rest. This complete practice was repeated and repeated until the instructors were fully satisfied with our confidence and expertise.

Our training also involved understanding the ejection of the soul body from each physical carcass as the drowning took place. On the day, we would not be dealing with corpses, but 'live' etheric counterparts in a state of shock and confusion. They would also be floating gently up to the surface, but they would be speaking to us in thought, and may even protest at our presence. That may sound strange since they had drowned and should be grateful to be rescued, but they would not necessarily be aware they were 'dead'! Grabbing a body was one thing, but dealing with bewilderment and resentment was another!

7.1.05 - 9.22pm

Can you imagine for a moment lying on the beach in the sun feeling very relaxed, when all of a sudden the cry of alarm goes up as the first monster wave is seen coming towards shore. Panic, terror, frenzy! You have no time to get away as moments later you are engulfed in the overwhelming torrent! Your breathing is choked, your senses pass out, and your invisible soul body immediately ejects from your physicality. The first stage of death! Nature has provided this incredible 'back up body', a perfect replica of the earthly one, as an escape route out of your worldly life for the first stage into a new 'survival' into our heavenly dimensions.

9.50am

Thousands have made a part time pull-out during a heart attack, operation, severe coma or fever, but have been returned into their physical life to tell the tale. But in this particular case of the Tsunami drowning it was for real. In seconds you are in physical life one minute, and then floating and breathing through water the next! What would your reaction be? Pretty stunned I would imagine! And you wouldn't be alone. A few dozen others would be floating past you!

Then we turn up wearing snorkels, adding to the general drama and growing casualties floating around under the sea. As we firmly stretch out our arms to grab an arm, or slip them round a waist, if we're lucky, the protests begin:-

"What the hell's going on? Don't you dare grab me like that!" (And that is putting it mildly).

"Sorry to upset you lady, but we're here to help you back to safety"

"I don't need your help. I can swim! How do I know you're not some male molester taking advantage of me?"

"You don't to be honest, but if you care to look upwards you'll see a beautiful radiance shining down upon you from Heaven"

"Heaven! What are you talking about? I'm having a bad dream, that's what! Go away so I can wake up!"

Well we couldn't float around arguing the matter, our instructions were to carry them all, kicking and screaming if necessary, onto a raft as quickly as possible, where they would be immediately sedated to forget the trauma for some time. They would all wake up in Heaven much later and much calmer. Meantime, as each lay in a raft, the fine umbilical chord which was still attached to the physical carcass, would snap and dissolve with the help of a medical expert on board. Each rescued soul was then free from physical life altogether.

(break - 10.33am)

You might ask at this point what we were doing wearing snorkels if we could breathe under the sea like the drowned victims in their ejected soul bodies. You're right, but we needed to wear them to distinguish us as the rescuers, as opposed to those needing rescuing. There would be enough confusion in the water, so this was our 'uniform' as you might say. Also, the glass porthole of the snorkel was our special screen of clarity to view the Earth world in perfect focus as we carried out the rescue operation under the sea.

Another question you might ask is, why we did not let them all make their own way to safety? Well to where? Remember, they were still within the earthly vibrations, and we would have had to lower ours considerably beforehand to reach out to them for the rescue. The turbulent sea was flooding everywhere inland, there was no beach left at that point. If they had made it back to shore as new invisible spirits now, their bewilderment would have been even greater because no-one would see them on Earth anymore. They would perceive the devastation around them, and have no means to do anything about it, ending up earthbound and stranded in an alien landscape completely smashed by the torrent, until other rescuers came to persuade them to turn to the light and help them to go forward into their true place in the heavenly Realms. Far better we pushed them into the full change there and then. You'll see why later.

9.1.05 - 2.22pm

As for the dark tunnel, which is often described in near death experiences, in this particular disaster this phase was obliterated by such a huge mass of passing into Spirit almost simultaneously. The reason being, that our mass presence within the rescue operation creates an enormous deluge of soul consciousness in one accord. The continuous healing radiance shining down in protective upliftment from Heaven, before, during and for some months afterwards, opened the 'doors' very wide for a universal transference into the higher dimensions when the rescue work was complete. As the last new soul was gently laid on a raft we would be 'airlifted' as you might say, en mass, into the lower heavenly domains with all those we had safely collected from Earth.

Well, that just about sums up the preparation training and information we all went through before waiting for the dreaded reality, which came all too soon!

We were positioned in large ships hours in advance of the underwater earthquake eruption. On board we tried to relax amongst each other while waiting in anxious trepidation. Each ship was moored mid-ocean near to its designated area for rescue. Ours and others were lined up for the coast of Thailand.

As the first rumblings were monitored on our screens, we were lined up on deck like an army inspection parade to check we had everything we needed. The minutes ticked by as we were lowered vibrationally into the earthly atmosphere, which is pretty dense mentally compared with our very light, uplifting frequencies in the Summerlands. It was a bit like being lowered inside a submarine into the depths of the ocean, and feeling the strong pressure all around. During this short interval the vision of Heaven was blanked out, and we had to wait until we reached the Earth atmosphere before the new scene opened up to us. Almost immediately we felt the first swell of the ocean beneath the boat building up from the earthquake.

Our ship was moving forward towards its destination. Suddenly, without any warning, we were pitched into the sea a short way from the shore as the boat nearly capsized from the power of the waves! It was such a shock as we struggled in the water to gain our balance, mount our surfboards and go for it. Dozens of white water rafts were dumped over the side of the ship with their own trained experts to sail them safely behind us over the choppy water between high waves! Some of these, with special divers on board, would overtake us beyond the beach area to raft over the swirling rapids of the surging torrent flooding inland over streets, hotel complexes and towns farther inland, to collect their Earth victims.

It all happened so quickly we didn't have time to think except to concentrate upon keeping our balance as we reared up the last huge wave as its ridge curled over to begin crashing hard towards the beach ahead. I just about managed to hang on as I surfed above the foam before diving into the swirling waters to seek my first soul body for rescue. I was joined by a hundred or so others with the same motive in mind!

We dived into unbelievable chaos! Bodies flying in all directions! You just didn't know where to start. Then the miracle happened! Like a fast movie camera slowing down, the scene before us changed into a tranquil undulation of detail, which became easily discernable. Instead of a raging ocean tearing everyone apart, there was a clear line-up of soul bodies floating quietly up to the surface. It was Heaven's amazing magic to help us carry out our rescue operation in peace and quiet. Heaven had purposely slowed down her 'clocks' to allow us 'real time' for our task.

With little difficulty I cradled a little child in my arms, and took her to a raft. Several more followed. The first lady I swam up to was a little panic stricken, but I managed to calm her enough to put my arm around her waist, and the other under her legs to lift her to the raft. She soon fell asleep.

Next came two men, who were somewhat resentful of my presence. Who did I think I was grabbing them by the hands? Each tried to fight me off. I hung on trying to explain my purpose. They wouldn't believe me! My nearest companion in the water came to my rescue, a young female surfer. That did the trick, and between us we escorted each one to a raft.

Later, an old lady was really sweet, and seemed to be quite resigned to my help. Having deposited her onto a raft, I went back into the water one more time. It appeared to be empty...or was it? Some way off I caught sight of another small child drifting towards me from beyond the beach inland. Amazingly the little lad floated directly into my arms. He looked up at me very quizzically as if to say "What's happening?" He would have been too young on Earth to speak normally, but in his new soul body he could communicate his feelings very plainly. I held him to me while boarding the raft, and cradled him in my arms as we waited for the signal to ascend to Heaven.

Meantime, the other white water rafters, who had sailed beyond the beach inland, were still collecting their 'survivors' either in the waves, or from the flooded and ruined buildings smashed from the weight and frenzy of the turbulent waves. Their task was more difficult while reaching out to the ejected soul bodies, who found themselves above the debris and were floundering in complete bewilderment. Flooded swimming pools were searched for more adults and children floating up to the surface. It seemed never ending, until at last the signal came for departure.

The terrible scenes were blanked out as we ascended into Heaven once more, but leaving behind countless other volunteers who were remaining in the earthbound wavelengths to help with the emergency work in physical life. We will hear about them next.

I cannot describe the relief and joy as the brilliant scene of the Summerlands came into focus for us all. There we were gently riding the shallow waves towards a beautiful tropical beach, and ahead, waiting on the sands were hundreds of past relatives of the victims ready to welcome each one when they awoke. It was a very moving sight as each rescued etheric soul was gently laid to rest under the palms with a loving family member sitting beside them to take their hand, smooth their brow and surround them with flowers, fruit and gifts.

My little lad was handed over to his own great granny and aunt, who each kissed him tenderly on the cheeks, tears rolling down their own, and then thanked me profusely for his safe rescue. I was in tears myself in relief of the trauma, as I sat down to rest with them for a while.

In the many days to come, these new arrivals would slowly wake up to see the sand, sea and palm trees all around, smiling faces looking down on them, and feel complete calm and peace as though nothing had happened at all". (4.55pm)

Part Two

SUPPORTING THE AFTERMATH ON EARTH

12th January 2005 8.04pm

"Can you hear me?"

"Yes, your voice is coming through. Thank you for communicating."

"I'm calling you from an aircraft resembling a large helicopter flying over the whole area of the Indian Ocean Earthquake Zone. We are as close to the earthbound vibrations as we can get, and are taking a wide 'birds eye view' of the general devastation all around resulting from the terrible eruption. Already your physical world has responded well to the S.O.S. for help. But there are many problems to overcome in the weeks ahead, which we can foresee in advance.

As I speak to you, we are high enough to view the general colouring of the water-torn landscapes, from Thailand and Indonesia in the East, to Sri Lanka, India and the Maldive Islands to the West. All the main territories and many small islands badly hit by the high waves thundering onto the land. We are flying silently and unseen by your eyes on Earth, and carry the most advanced equipment for geographical surveillance to perceive the details of the devastation, plus magnified telepathic and emotional pick-up perception from the stricken population on the ground far below.

Our reconnaissance is to ascertain all the needs of your survivors and helpers, where there is help, where there isn't help, what kind of help is needed, how this can be instigated, and how well help is already being achieved. Our super-sensitive monitors pick up signals and information beamed to us from the various vibration levels on Earth, such as individual thought patterns, community motivation, group endeavour, emergency alarms, hysteria, terror, anguish, shock, pain, grief, and in particular 'feed back' received from our enormous contingencies of souls helping all they can on ground level *unseen*!

I am the Chief Emergency Commander for this catastrophe, and wish to explain all our very exacting mental labours in every aspect of supporting human endeavour, towards gaining some measure of comfort and improvement in the overwhelming chaos following the Tsunami destruction.

Our work began prior to the eruption, not only in the now stricken areas, but all around the world among leaders and politicians, who would be the ones to organise the emergency relief programmes. Every national leader is shadowed by more than one guide or relative from our dimensions, every appropriate aid and charitable organisational headquarters is shadowed by a team of our representatives, and every family with a likely victim from the disaster is given very special spirit counsellors, plus comforters from their own spirit relatives.

Our planning beforehand is the most intricate schedule imaginable. Everything and everybody must be firmly in place well in advance of the terrible happening. Our aim initially is to save as many lives as possible in the onslaught. Our aim immediately after the event is to rally the emergency help as quickly as possible. As the days and weeks pass, our aim is to direct everyone's minds in physical life towards the smoothest rescue operation, the deepest comfort, and a deep commitment towards a rehabilitation programme.

As the Tsunami struck Earth, your greatest disadvantage was having to cope with the speed and devastation of people, buildings, towns and landscape all being annihilated so quickly with hardly any warning! So to try to offset this shock of such an unpredictable catastrophe, the Highest Realms of Heaven in the Sphere of Light sent an enormous strength of healing radiance into your physical wavelengths to considerably boost the general moral and mental resilience of everyone caught in one capacity or another within the disaster area. Vibration levels of health and vitality are heightened in advance, plus mental alertness, mental courage and emotional strength of mind.

Long before your Christmas, the radiance of loving Light was descending into the Indian Ocean Zone in readiness, and also around the families of potential casualties, suitable emergency organisations, and world leaders in other parts of your world. In many senses, the Christmas festivities of love and goodwill was an extra blessing aiding the pre-eruption upliftment. The happy moods over the Christmas period boosted the 'Silver Lining' from heaven.

You have already received a description of the surfing rescue operation, which was repeated many times in the different areas near to the epicentre of the under water ocean earthquake. Our own contingent of helpers were also on hand, at the same time, in our role to infiltrate as much emergency thought inspiration as possible into the minds and hearts of men, women and children struggling to find every possible means of escape to safety, or helping others likewise; and to amplify the initial shouts of alerting the approaching danger as the torrential waves bore down towards them and flood inland. Survivors have lived to tell their awesome tales. Those who were unscathed and in a position to lend a helping hand were catapulted into action straight away by their individual spirit co-ordinators.

In short, once our alarm bells rang loud and clear, the huge network of our aid helpers were prompted into immediate interchange of lightening-fast thought one to another. The speed of thought for us in Heaven is instant, the same as it is for you, but for us it is freer and clearer to travel without any restriction of a slow physical body in comparison. The telepathic communication between our supporters for you was so rapid that none of your computers, telephone or radio systems would in any way be able to keep up the momentum! *(9.12pm)*

19.01.06 - 7.05pm

Time is also on our side. Unlike your world we can slow down our so-called 'clocks' to stretch the availability of emergency action to a maximum. What may be seconds and minutes to you became ten, twenty and thirty minutes to us, and if necessary hours to carry out intricate schedules of help and support. For those suffering pain and agonising injuries, waiting hopelessly for comfort, or those stranded unable to free themselves and also waiting for help, we speed the time up, so it only seems a very short while before they are attended to on Earth.

Many women in your world find this happens during childbirth. The intense pain of the contractions seems interminable at the time, but when the baby is safely born the new mother is often surprised at the true length of time it took to make the delivery. A day's labour upon reflection may only seem like a short while as she looks back in memory. The terrible pain is quickly forgotten in the joy of cradling the new baby in her arms.

In this enormous tragedy, the retrieval of the multitudes of dead bodies was perhaps the most arduous labour, and indeed the most upsetting for all parties involved. We cannot underestimate this enormous task on Earth, as you will agree from your own many reports, and we cannot describe the weight of responsibility for all our carers, who painstakingly guided your teams of hard endeavour, to collect and locate as many as possible for those who were desperately seeking survival of their loved ones in physical life.

The anguish and torment was monitored very deeply in our dimensions motivating more radiance and healing rays to be infiltrated into your atmosphere, wherever it was needed, to try to cushion the demented spirits of the devoted families pleading for news of their loved ones caught in the disaster areas.

Many of our convent sisters and monastic monks were present in the hospitals and make-shift camps to administer a soothing strength of mind for all those in shock, pain and grief. Losing one loved one is bad enough, but to lose a whole family is very deeply distressing and a personal tragedy likely to wound the heart for life.

Apart from meeting those who had passed into our dimensions

from drowning, past relatives attached to all the casualties were divided between Heaven and Earth. Some remained within our vibration levels to comfort the so-called 'dead', and others were on hand to comfort and support those in need throughout your own devastated aftermath.

The complication of so much disorder due to the enormous need for help all at once, was monitored very closely and carefully by our contingencies of helpers close to your wavelengths. They volunteered from all cultures and creeds in unity of purpose to uplift humanity in such serious need. Many ex-doctors and nurses from our lower Heaven took it upon themselves to be present in all the make-shift hospitals, and indeed any other major hospital, which took in the countless injured victims. Their main task was to co-ordinate as much inspiration as possible to aid the poor and crowded conditions of the patients, and to bring utmost strength and endurance to bear upon the teams of medical staff, working round the clock, to do all they could for the sick and injured.

Food relief for the starving populations, cut off from their normal supplies, was allocated particular importance. Your own contingencies of imported supplies, were very strongly shadowed by land, air and sea, as well as for each localised inland city and town also stretching out a helping hand wherever possible. In short, wherever there was a need, we were there to help it along, and, if political deadlocks held up progress, our negotiators worked overtime to try to convince the minds of the arbitrators that the emergency was far greater than their selfish ideals.

I have talked long enough about the various aspects of our general presence among you on Earth, encouraging every progress possible in the aftermath of this unexpected terrible catastrophe. We will touch down to ground now, to allow you to see for yourselves one or two examples of our work in practice. Perhaps the worst hit area was Bande Aceh very close to the epicentre of the earthquake. Complete devastation! We will go back in time to the immediate hours following the flooding and its destruction.

We are slowly dropping down to the area in hand. While we do so let me explain a little more about myself, and this aircraft I am piloting. My original career on Earth was an officer in the army during the Second World War, during which we became used to the devastation as the bombs dropped, and the guns fired to kill the enemy. Bodies everywhere! I arrived in these Realms in the middle of it all, and was pretty confused myself for sometime. But in a way it prepared me for this kind of rescue work in Spirit. When I had settled in and joined other teams on disaster projects, I was offered training in the airforce to expand my experience. This I accepted readily as a change from operating solely on the land. I also did a stint in the navy for a while to gain complete overall understanding. So here I am now in a very responsible position to oversee all areas of our rescue supporting teams.

24.01.05 - 7.12pm

Our aircraft is descending very slowly so we can observe the details of the Tsunami destruction far below, section by section, through the means of a telepathic scanner positioned underneath the helicopter, and aligned centrally to the cockpit above.

The 'photographed' reflections are vibrationally recorded on our monitor screen, and are powered by thought wavelengths. We are, as it were, mapping out the total devastation of the Bande Aceh area and beyond, while at the same time picking up all the distress signals from the human anguish and suffering of those who have initially survived, plus the newly ejected souls after drowning. Any difficulties registering from the surfing teams are brought into close up focus, if necessary, and given the due attention they need from other helpers in the same area concerned. On the ground it is a form of 'mobile phone' communication via pure thought travel at very high speed.

A team of experts in this telepathic signalling are aboard this special helicopter, deciphering and analysing all the incoming information continually, and sending out the required help and answers to the problems being encountered on ground level by our spirit team infiltrating as much inspiration and upliftment as possible. The outer casing of this aircraft is an ultra fine resin beautifully shaped and designed in a shining white form, which can be seen like a beacon in the sky emanating a radiance of healing light for a considerable distance in diameter, over the whole of the Indian Ocean Zone needing emergency help.

My co-pilot and I control this flight from a cockpit that is a mastery of simple telepathic techniques. If we think in our minds the command, "Please cruise ahead", the beautiful craft obeys instantaneously, and in the same way reacts obediently if we reduce or excel speed, forwards, backwards or downwards. Distance is measured in vibration wavelengths and fed into a monitor at our request. Its 'fuel' is the ether through which it travels, which is purified and recycled upon entry into our 'fuel' system. Once again this is monitored carefully by thought intention to use only enough 'fuel' necessary for each manoeuvre and not give way to any wastage. There are no intoxicating emissions whatsoever, and no trails of pollution. In short it is silent, efficient, graceful, and a joy to pilot wherever our mission takes us.

We are now ready to touch down onto the land, very, very gently in an open space, where we can camouflage our aircraft in any way required if necessary. Its outer colour can change according to the landscapes so as not to be intrusive to those in our dimensions, who value their surroundings very deeply. However, they are always informed of our arrival in advance. In this particular case, we seek to land on the calmer sea using our water stabilisers to hover above the surface very smoothly. Some of the rescuers need a helping hand. They are in need of our special healing radiance to calm the new spirit souls from agitation. One or two of our individuals on board are disembarking wearing diving suits to join a group of surfers to offer them special nose masks of sweet-scented aromas to tranquilise their charges very gently, and lull them into a reverie of peace. *(8.14pm)*

26.01.05 - 7.50pm

Our first mission completed, we gently rise up above the land and buildings inland to scour the area for rescue difficulties. People clinging to bars, caught in trees, or hanging on to anything that is nearest to them in order to keep them above water! Our white-water rafters are keeping up their moral until physical help comes their way, and the tide begins to recede. The radiance from our aircraft permeates the atmosphere as much as possible, which may not be felt directly on Earth, but without it there would be far more anguish, terror and panic.

The lucky ones able to escape in one form or another from the overwhelming torrent, but receiving minor wounds from the backlash of debris swirling in the waters, are given heightened strength and endurance to keep going until they are truly out of the worst danger. This is the time of the disaster when the tick-tack communication between spirit helpers, operating close to the Earth vibrations, starts in earnest to bring the nearest help and support to the victims as soon as possible. It is like a wave of rippling telepathy travelling into every corner of the disaster scenes, weaving an intricate network of signalling to converge with the emergency help.

Searching for the bodies became an all consuming emergency operation for days and weeks afterwards. Once again, no stone was left unturned by our teams to co-ordinate a unity of endeavour on Earth as our dimensions looked down on the terrible scenes. The harrowing grief of bereavement created an overwhelming cloud of deep distress, 'above and below'. Every individual registering their shock and sorrow as a loved one, or more, were confirmed dead or missing, were shadowed in love and compassion immediately, and are still being slowly guided through their devastating grief for months, and perhaps years, to regain some sense of stability. Every family member, or members, standing before the sea of photos on the never ending boards was given an invisible helper and consoler from our Realms. The orphaned children in particular, some losing whole families, were given unseen nannies and angelic spirit children to sit by them in comfort, day and night. Fostering them with the right individuals or families on Earth will be our prime target as the months pass in your time. Sadly, they are particularly vulnerable to abuse, which shocks us as deeply in Heaven as it does you on Earth, but the outcomes will be resolved with your strong co-operation too.

Finally, we turn our attention to the sick and injured in the crowded hospitals. Our heavenly helicopter touches down completely in a large devastated area of rubble. The team of men and women on board disperse, by projecting themselves in thought to the nearest hospital as chief co-ordinators, to support the existing contingency team already struggling to infuse practical thought and action to all the hospital staff. Many patients are already dying from chronic wounds and shock! Each ejected soul is lovingly lifted into our higher Realms, where loved ones await by their beds in our very lovely convalescent centres. They may pass from your life in crowded emergency conditions, but they will 'wake up' in peace and luxury in Heaven, and receive all the attention they could wish for.

Meantime as the many imported doctors and nurses struggle to comfort the distressed casualty victims in the make-shift wards in physical life, our teams of doctors and nurses shadow them very closely. The patients are also cared for by them alongside a close relative in our vibrations. None lie alone in their suffering, and none are left for a moment until they are fully recovered from Earth, and reunited with loved ones again. Our experienced aircraft team members carry very small portable computer style calculators, which work out all the most favourable possibilities of generating help and removing the obstacles and difficulties towards successful outcomes.

For instance, if a nurse is struggling to find a bed for another badly injured patient being brought in by an orderly, because every square foot is already covered by a mass of other patients on beds, one of our nearest team members will tick-tack to the nearest spirit helper in another department of the dilemma. They in turn will tick-tack to yet another helper nearest to an earthly hospital doctor or superintendent of the alarming situation. Each inquiry is explaining the urgency, and asking if they are near anyone in physical life that can help? This complete round of appeal will last seconds in your time! Meantime, the pocket calculator in the hands of our operator is surveying the emergency situation for the best solution. The main object is to find bed space. The computer mind studies the layout of the hospital, which we relay from our own information system on board the helicopter at its request, and suggestions are fed to our team operator.

By chance, or so it seems on Earth, a hospital orderly comes forward to summon a nurse that a space is available temporarily in another room or corridor, while they open up a veranda for further bed occupations. What may have lasted some while on Earth was resolved far quicker by our helpers, but the time involved in negotiating the minds of the hospital staff took far longer to achieve.

Finally, as the immediate emergency problems begin to be resolved, and some form of progress is made while your days and weeks pass, our aircraft will remain unseen to iron out the numerous set-backs and problems as they occur. As chief co-ordinator I am in contact with dozens of other similar aircraft hovering over their specially designated areas. Some of them will cruise beside the airliners of your world, which are making their way to land safely with food, supplies and medical first aid. Our ships will also escort yours to their destinations of help and support.

In conclusion, our heavenly dimensions and your physical world become as one under the sole purpose of bringing love, compassion and expert aid to the mass of victims suffering the many torments on Earth, following this terrible Tsunami earthquake catastrophe. I do hope my words and explanation bring some small measure of insight and comfort to you all. We are forever with you." *(9.35pm)*

Part Three

THE AWAKENINGS IN HEAVEN

2nd February 2005 8.03pm

"Hello, can you hear me, Sigrid?"

"Yes, I am surprised to hear from you Petal."

"You are always remembering me in your prayers, and I wanted to let you know that I am with you, more than you realise. We had a wonderful understanding together on spiritual matters."

"We did indeed. It was always lovely seeing you."

"I've been chosen to relate this episode because my voice is familiar to you, and we had a good rapport. As you know I was a nurse in Canada years ago, which I had to leave to look after my mother in London during the last war. She and I have come together in these Realms to offer our services of love and compassion. On our journey among the new souls awakening from the ocean earthquake disaster, we shall meet others carrying out their service of love and care.

I'm speaking to you from a very beautiful nursing home, which is known here as a Reception Recovery Centre. There are many dozens of similar buildings in this special Rescue Realm, which have been created to accommodate the many thousands of casualties from your world. They are looked after in great comfort, and have many visitors coming to see them. All their past relatives, all their past friends, and all their past work associates. My own nursing care has been to explain to them about what has happened, and to help them to come to terms with their new existence in the Summerland's, the Third Sphere of Heaven. I am meeting men and women from various parts of the world, as well as numerous children from India, Sri Lanka, Thailand and so on, as I travel from one Reception Centre to another.

When the drowned victims first arrived from Earth, they were laid out under the palms of the beautiful sandy beaches in this Realm. They remained asleep for some days, even for over a week in your time in some cases. Their closest relatives or friends stayed by their sides in quiet vigil. So we didn't have much to do at that stage, except walk up and down the beach in our nursing teams to inspect the new patients from time to time.

During this waiting period we came into contact with higher authority figures, who would appear every so often to bring true heavenly wisdom and compassion onto the scene.

These were Brothers and Sisters of Light, offering their long experience in rescue work to those of us who were being initiated into this specialised vocation. Christian convent sisters and monastic monks were among them. Also many Buddhist monks, Indian ladies wearing colourful saris, Indonesian Muslims and Indian Hindus. All would walk together in conversation and friendship without a hint of prejudice! In the Highest Realms of Heaven all religions, as you understand them on Earth, are completely at one with each other. Only the colours and styles of their robes and garments distinguish them from their various cultures.

The ladies working in my nursing team were of mixed nationalities, which I found very interesting and broadened my own outlook very much. The Indian women wearing the lovely saris were particularly gentle and understanding towards everyone, but especially to our patients in Heaven. They were a true example of tender care and dedication bringing comfort and upliftment to the new bewildered souls as they awoke, and the true reality dawned upon them. But the supreme example to us all was the beloved Jesus.

He appeared one day, soon after the catastrophe, at the end of our particular beach. I just happened to look up from a half awake patient in my charge as he slowly made his way down the long, long line of new souls lying peacefully on the soft golden sands under the palm trees. Around him was the most beautiful soft radiance distinguishing him from the other white robed figures walking beside him. I was so thrilled to be given the honour of seeing him at close hand as he eventually drew very near, a couple of patients away from me. At this point he was bending down to speak to an Indonesian lady, who was looking up at him in anxiety, not quite knowing what was happening and why she was there. With the relatives' kind permission, he sat down beside her very calmly and took her hand. *(9.14pm)*

5.2.05 - 8.36pm

His eyes looked towards mine as if to say "Please listen to our conversation so you may learn from the words, and pass it on to others in due course. I bless you dear sister for your help in this aftermath from the Earth tragedy." I returned my thoughts to him in deep thanks for the privilege, and then watched very carefully as he smoothed her brow very gently for a few minutes while gazing very kindly into her eyes. She responded very quickly to his loving caress as her agitation calmed down, and she lay back in renewed relaxation. Then the conversation began.

"My dearest lady, what is disturbing you on this beautiful beach under the palm trees? Are you not comfortable?"

She hesitated for a minute or so, not quite sure what to say.

"I am very comfortable", she replied in thought of her own language, which was automatically translated for whoever was listening from the vibrational wavelengths of a transmitter, which were silently circulating among patients and helpers alike. The surrounding ethers were fully programmed to understand all the likely languages and dialects in this Rescue Realm. As each conversation resonated in the air, this miraculous telepathic system picked up the words from the speaker and delivered them to the recipient in perfect understanding of their own tongue, if it was different from the speakers language. It was so instantaneous that you felt everyone was speaking your native tongue. There was also a central building further inland, which was transmitting the wavelengths continuously to smaller monitors hidden among the palms. A team of language experts were monitoring the whole procedure from this central building.

The Indonesian lady went on to explain her feelings to the Lord.

"When I awoke I wondered where I was for a while, and then I noticed many others like me all lying under the palm trees, and other people gazing at us as they passed by. Why are we here Sir?" She gazed hard into his face for an answer.

"My dear lady, you are in very good hands and being cared for very deeply by our nursing assistants and doctors along this beach, and your own dear relatives by your side. You are here to recover from a deep traumatic shock, from which you have been sedated for a while".

"I still don't understand, where are we?"

"You are on a tropical beach very similar to the one you lived close to a few days ago. Do you remember it?"

"No, not at the moment. Will I be going back soon?"

"Alas, not for the time being. And if you desire to return later, it will be in a new way than before."

He held her hand at this point more firmly. She became agitated again.

"We've got to get away! We've got to get away! The water's coming! The waves! The waves!!" Her voice died away as she slumped back as if she had passed out.

During this quiet interlude, Jesus remained by her side knowing she would wake again to further revelations. Meantime, a young Christian orderly came up to the Lord, having been told of his presence with this Indonesian lady, and asked his advice.

"Lord, I have been told that most of these casualties are Muslims. I was expecting to look after Christians, who have come to Heaven from this terrible catastrophe! Surely I should be with my own religious people. Lord, I see this woman you are tending is a Muslim. She is not a Christian."

"She is a woman in need and that is all that matters."

"But she..." The young man was very quickly, but gently interrupted.

34

"There are no 'buts', dear brother, only the love and compassion of our hearts", came the emphatic reply.

"Lord, I still do not understand why you have chosen to be in this Indonesian area of the Rescue Realm, and not with the Christian sector?"

"There is no Christian sector, my friend. All are mixed together at random. This dear lady may be a Muslim, but further down the beach there are some Christians amongst Hindus, Buddhists and other Muslims. Heaven has no religious prejudices, and neither should you. I choose to bring my healing balm to them all. Was not my teaching on Earth to love your neighbour as yourself. I was a Jew at the time, and still am in nationality. But in relevance to Christianity, which was propagated after I departed from Earth, I remain it's figurehead. However, during the many centuries of my sojourn in Heaven, I have grieved deeply that my followers have not entirely grasped the fundamentals of my teachings. *(9.50pm)* Apart from the bickering amongst each other and between their denominations, killings and atrocities have been carried out in the name of my faith, as well as civil wars against other creeds, and worse still against their own kind, as in Ireland. What pride does this bring to my name and heart? It is only the good works and devotion on the part of countless sincere individuals over the ages, who have reconciled my mind to the true cause of Christianity. My dear young man, you will find our ways in Heaven are very different, and I am present on this scene merely as a brotherly support to my Muslim colleagues, and every other creed represented in this aftermath from the ocean earthquake catastrophe."

The Christian orderly fell silent for a few moments hearing these words from Jesus. He could find no answer, only another question that came to his mind.

"Why did this terrible tragedy happen. Has God the Father no mercy?"

"You see His deep mercy before you in this Rescue Realm of care and compassion, and indeed in the courage and fortitude of those, who lifted these new souls from the tempestuous waters on Earth, to lay them to rest in our dimensions under the palms."

"But God the Father should never have let it happen in the first place!"

"Dear brother, what choice did He have in the matter. A planet which is faulted beneath the sea, the shifting movements of its crust, and human beings living perilously close to any likely eruption? It should never have been allowed to place these people in such danger!"

"I see what you mean Lord, but even so, many people will lose faith in God."

"Alas they will, but in time they will come to understand that His intention is never to bring any calamity into their midst. He is entirely at the mercy of the intentions and actions of human beings. He cannot dictate to their lives without taking away their so called 'free will'. Mankind must work alongside God to create a better, safer world."

"I don't quite understand, Lord?"

"The beautiful Earth environment is being plundered for its natural resources, its landscape being decimated continuously, and the ravages of war not far from the Indian Ocean Zone in recent times have brought untold violation in huge explosives setting off vibrational reverberations into the very soil of the Earth, which in turn creates minor rumblings in themselves. The weakness of the planet's structure becomes very vulnerable to all these atrocities, and once in a while gives way! Mankind must learn to honour the beauty and riches of God's planet."

Once again the young orderly fell silent for some minutes, then unexpectedly fell down on his knees before Jesus.

"Beloved Lord, I accept all that you say in simple wisdom, which speaks now to my heart. I thank you for the privilege to question you on these matters. I beg I may be of service to you in this new example of love. I feel I am just awakening myself like these casualties, even though I have been in Heaven a short while.

I was 'blind' and now I 'see'!"

"Praise be to God the Father and Mother of us all for bringing you to me. Our dear Indonesian lady is stirring again. If you would care to join me for a while to witness my attention to her, you may indeed learn a little more in compassion towards your fellow human souls. I accept your offer of kind service on condition you continue likewise, on your own, among your other comrades offering help in this domain, and pass on my words to whoever else seeks the same answers as yourself."

"With all my heart, beloved Lord. I realise now we all need many awakenings in Heaven to understand the true meaning of God's Love."

"We do indeed dear brother". *(4.15pm)*

9.2.05 - 9.10pm

As I watched this scene and listened to the conversation between the dear Lord and the young Christian orderly, I remembered all my own teaching on Earth with Unity Church, which seemed quite relevant in the light of this beautiful humble understanding from Jesus himself. I was very moved by the young man's final 'conversion' to Jesus' revelations of God's Love. But this was just the beginning of his many informal teachings as he made his way down the long lines of new souls awakening along our beach, plus the many he personally visited. I heard from friends and colleagues later of further short discussions he exchanged between carers and patients.

The Indonesian lady was now wide awake again, and asking more questions of the Lord, who was still holding her hand in strength and comfort. The young man was seated beside him watching intently as the next sequel unfolded.

"Do you feel a little calmer, my dear lady?"

"A little, but I feel very afraid deep down inside. I don't know why?"

"Then just try to enjoy the lovely surroundings for the moment. We have all the time in the world to help you feel more at ease."

"Why are all these other people here like me?"

"They too have had a similar shock like you."

"What was it that happened?" She tightened her grip of his hand.

"Far away on another beach, huge tidal waves engulfed you completely. You are quite safe here."

Her face became very alarmed again, staring up into his eyes in fear again. She grabbed his arm in panic! "It mustn't happen again. I don't want it to happen again!"

"It's alright, my dear lady. Nothing will happen again, I do assure you." There was a pause as the Lord concentrated his healing radiance upon her.

"Did you rescue me?" She asked in quieter tones.

"No, not personally, but someone else helped you to this shore."

"Where are we?"

"You are in Heaven dearest lady!" She let out a loud groan of horror as she clasped her hand to her mouth. She could not speak for several minutes.

"I'm dead!"

"You are alive in Heaven!"

"I'm dead!" She repeated, "I'm dead?" She questioned in disbelief.

"Yes, but you are alive and well," confirmed the Lord. He gestured to the orderly to find a stretcher to bear the lady to one of the many waiting ambulances beyond the palms, to take her to a Reception Convalescent Centre farther away for further rest and recuperation. This was her initial awakening to our dimensions, but she would have several more sleeps with some number of awakenings, until the full realisation had sunk into her mind.

By now she had passed out again, and the dear Lord lifted her gently onto the stretcher when it arrived, plucked a beautiful blossom from one of the flowering Hibiscus bushes along the edge of the beach, and laid it in one of her hands. He made the sign of a cross on her forehead in blessing before she was carried to the ambulance with loving relatives by her side.

"It will take her time, dear brother, to reconcile her mind to the change of circumstances, because it came so suddenly without warning. They will all take time to adjust to this dimension, and it is the next stage of the awakening, which will demand much patience and deep understanding to help them all through to stability and acceptance. It will not be easy. The shock of the immediate change into a new existence will unbalance their emotions for a while. They will become resentful and angry to have had their lives cut short from Earth, and many tears will be shed at leaving loved ones behind". He explained to the young orderly still beside him. "Shall we move on to the next patient together?"

"Whatever you say, Lord. I'll follow you wherever you wish."

"I suggest you stay with me for a few more patients before joining your own colleagues farther up the beach. A little more experience will stand you in good stead. No one person reacts the same as another, as you will discover."

"I understand Lord. Thank you for allowing me to come with you."

12.2.05 - 8.40pm

At this moment they both stopped in their tracks in front of me and my own patient with loved ones beside her. The Lord gestured for me to come to him and stretched out his hand to clasp mine.

"Peace of Heaven be with you, dearest lady and carer. Our deepest gratitude for your loving help and support in this Rescue Realm".

"Thank you, beloved Lord, for allowing me to listen to your own wonderful compassion of understanding. It has inspired me very much."

"Then I do hope you will pass it on in communication to a past friend on Earth. I will send an experienced communicator to you for assistance in the task."

"I will be greatly honoured, dear Lord."

"The privilege is mine, dear lady, to honour the work of all those who have willingly offered to undertake such commitment. We could not do without any one of you. I bid you farewell for another time. Heaven's blessing be upon you."

As he and the young orderly walked up the beach, I could hardly concentrate on what I was needing to do in the personal joy of receiving the Lord's thanks and blessing. His humble gratitude towards everyone he stopped to thank touched all our hearts. I shall remember those moments forever." *(9.00pm)*

Part Four

CONFUSION, GRIEF AND ANGER

12th February 2005. 9.10pm

"Greetings dear lady, may I speak to you?"

"You can indeed. It's taken a few minutes since I completed the last part to tune into the next voice. My greetings to you."

"I am a doctor and psychiatrist from India and therefore I am familiar with this part of the world. We are doing our very best to bring comfort to so many disturbed patients after the overwhelming shock of this Tsunami disaster. But first, I wish to describe to you the development of the Reception Centres and other buildings, while the casualties from Earth were sleeping after the shock.

This vast area of the Rescue Realm has been created from the natural ether in our atmosphere through thought manifestation. Experts first 'painted' the scenery, the landscape, the vegetation, the coastline and the sea beforehand. While the rescue work was taking place, the architects began to build the numerous Reception Centres, enough to house the thousands of new souls transported into our dimensions. Every design had been carefully planned weeks ahead in your time. It all took place like a fast moving film before your eyes! I came here before the disaster took place, and watched the amazing transformation as your days passed just before and during the horrific aftermath."

At the point of the renewed awakenings, all the victims from Earth were transferred to our Reception Convalescent Centres, one by one, from the beautiful beaches. They were then under close observation from our medical and counselling teams. We tried to keep as many family groups together as possible. This was a catastrophe which took whole communities into our Realms bringing much heartache and sorrow to all concerned. My task now is to help you all to understand that grief comes on both sides of the 'divide' between Heaven and Earth.

We are going to visit various wards and departments to try to give you all a general picture of the reaction of the new souls arriving in our dimension to the revelation of their death from the terrible ocean earthquake." *(9.50pm)*

20.2.05 - 3.10pm

But before we do so, I would like to explain that every soul arriving in these Realms of the afterlife from death in your world will be given a Life Review, once they have accepted their new environment. No individual is exempt except very young children passing over in distressing conditions. Their spirit minds will not be mature enough, and their suffering at the hands of human adults creates further mental blockages. These little ones are given every opportunity in Heaven to grow up normally in a very safe atmosphere, and develop all their natural talents to the full. This particular catastrophe brought untold thousands of children of all ages into our dimensions very suddenly and instantaneously, as you are all painfully aware. However, I must leave this specialised field to the communicator of the next section to follow mine.

Meantime, with regard to the adult sector of the disaster aftermath, the Life Review is compulsory, and has to be released fully, to allow the new soul full integration into the Spirit world. Their countless thoughts and actions throughout each life are 'video-taped' into the sub consciousness, and need to be brought to the surface in our domains to grant each individual soul a chance to assess their fulfilments and setbacks during physical life, in order to clear the way for a new start in wiser hindsight. The clarification and understanding of their true merits and discordances will also set the prospective vibratory field within which their soul can continue to exist most comfortably in our Realms. The Life Review is not so much to be feared as a severe judgement, but rather as a deep personal analysis to enlarge the perspective of one's own attitudes and shortcomings on the negative side, alongside the potential talents and gifts to be used in further experience in our dimensions on the positive side.

When each new soul has passed through this necessary examination of the past, it can move forward with greater awareness of his or her own needs towards expansion and progress in the new existence. It may even inspire a quite different way forward for new souls to express themselves in our Realms, hitherto hidden from their minds on Earth. In so doing, it will be very much a new start of intention, a new resolution of responsibility to themselves and others, and above all, a new life pattern built up from the mistakes made in the past, which are now put aside in the light of new aspirations.

20.2.05 - 8.56pm

However, in the wake of a catastrophic disaster on Earth such as this one, all the souls passing over in such a devastating tragedy are awarded special dispensations for their lives cut short so unexpectedly, over which they had no control. During each of their Life Reviews, those areas of their physical life which were questionable morally are postponed for examination at a much later date in their new heavenly lives.

Firstly, because they have suffered enough shock and trauma through the sudden disaster; secondly, because their lives have been cut short and therefore they have not been given the full term of maturity to perhaps put right any transgressions; and thirdly because God Himself feels bound to compensate their loss of life in the outcome of a so-called natural catastrophe, and to allow them all the time they need to balance their minds and hearts towards acceptance and integration of their new existence. As they follow their new paths in our dimensions, all their human frailties will come to light one by one, and it will be then that an opportunity will be given to them to look at these weaknesses in a much stronger frame of mind.

Let us now make our way into one of the Convalescent Reception Centres to view, at first hand, many of the new souls that passed into our domains from the Indian Ocean earthquake, and see and hear for yourselves their various stages of awakening and reaction to this new life in Heaven.

All our Reception Centres are very beautiful in architectural layout and throughout their interiors. They are very much like luxurious private hospitals on Earth. Bright airy rooms, many of them private suites, some catering for married couples, and many more are full family units with a series of inter-connecting rooms. Other wards can take up to four individuals for company and comfort together, while the children's wards are small dormitories with a play area for each child beside their bed, and a huge nursery playroom attached to each ward. Visiting relatives, already in our Realms, are given presidential treatment above friends and associates. Luxurious lounges act as comfortable waiting rooms, and every catering facility is provided inside, and also outside on gracious patios overlooking beautiful gardens and grounds.

Food and refreshment is of paramount importance for the patients as well as for hosting the many visitors. We may exist in invisible etheric realms beyond your physical sight, but we can still eat, sleep and exercise as on Earth, because our soul bodies are indeed perfect replicas of the worldly counterpart, and thought can manifest all these desires in perfect reality. However, nothing is allowed in excess. A strict balance is disciplined according to the true need of each individual. Heaven's monitoring system is conducted like an invisible consciousness tuned into every mind and heart, regulating all desires to their minimum or optimum threshold. *(9.47pm)*

21.2.05 - 7.10pm

In the wake of the traumatic Tsunami disaster the minds of all Earth casualties were numbed for some time. Their new spirit thoughts and awareness were greatly handicapped for a while, unable to differentiate between their own conflicting emotions and the new reality of love and comfort all around them.

When the first awakenings heralded the truth of their being in Heaven, their many reactions to their 'death' from physical life was marked shock and grief. Many slumped back into a coma of peaceful sleep before reawakening to finding themselves in a beautiful convalescent room, either on their own or with other casualties from their family or friends. The communal rooms proved to be a mixture of reunion and heartache. For most patients a comfort was to be found alongside loved ones they knew well in the same position as themselves, but not all members of the family or associate group would be present. Inevitably, some had been left behind on Earth, survivors in your world cut off now from those that once surrounded them. The grief on both sides was inconsolable!

All our very highly trained nurses, auxiliaries, counsellors, doctors and psychiatrists were working overtime to bring as much compassion and understanding to bear upon the harrowing scenes of bereavement. Hysteria and anger followed as the frustration of being unable to reconcile the situation set into their minds and hearts. Long experience over the centuries has taught us in Heaven to simply let each individual vent their anguish openly and in complete freedom, until they slowly calm down towards resignation. The deep emotions react in many different forms.

Some souls lie sullenly withdrawn for some time, some charge about ranting and raving, some just cry and sob unable to control the endless tears of tortuous sorrow. Some wander the grounds of the Convalescent Centre they are in trying to find a way of escape, and others over-eat, over-drink, over-talk and over-react to those who try hard to comfort them. Some have even been known to attack the helpers in their bottled up anger and rage over the inevitability of their passing.

This description may puzzle many of you who have become aware of the countless reports of near death experiences on Earth during which many of these men or women have 'out of body' experiences during a short interval of so-called death, and describe feeling such ecstasy and bliss with a strong desire to remain in this state. The bitter disappointment of coming back is deeply felt and unwanted. Why you may ask is it so different in this aftermath of the ocean earthquake catastrophe?

For one very good reason. There were thousands upon thousands passing over from very sudden death. This mass of consciousness had changed from physical to spiritual existence within seconds, perhaps minutes, some a little longer. The impact of such an enormously traumatic transition creates an equally enormous shock reaction, which has to release itself in whichever way it erupts according to the personalities of each new soul.

Nevertheless, Heaven's strong healing radiance and bliss will still permeate each individual soul throughout their transition, helping to sustain them in their moments of quieter calm, until it ultimately grows in strenth and stability.

25.2.05 - 7.34pm

No temperament from the physical life changes in Spirit. You are what you are on Earth and in Heaven. The only difference is that you will become younger in face and body, like a gradual change back to the age of your prime, if you were previously of mature physical years. If you were very young, or in your teens or twenties, you will just grow and develop your true potential towards your natural prime of life, and remain in that age for the rest of your time in Heaven, but hopefully gradually gaining greater maturity and wisdom in your mind and heart. Young people and children passing into Heaven have the distinct advantage of never growing old. *(10.11pm)*

When this difficult stage of disrupted consciousness passes, and each new soul finds a calmer frame of understanding and acceptance of the new outcome, the true experience of Heaven begins, and the loving radiance enfolding them quietly throughout their disturbed turmoil begins to grow and grow, until it engulfs their heart and soul in ultimate bliss and joy. God's unbounded love of compensation, following their personal tragedies, is their gift of natural martyrdom. Heaven opens all her doors to each one in endless opportunity to explore, enjoy, learn, relax and savour every blessed moment.

Alongside this new found joy, each individual soul will visit their earthbound loved ones in thought transportation to uplift them towards happiness once more, until both sides of the 'great divide' are at peace. In calmer stability, each one can move forward in their separate existences with a greater sense of life's fulfilments, until one day in the fullness of your own time on Earth, the ultimate reunion takes place as those left behind in physical existence pass over into Heaven, to reunite with their dear lost loved ones from this catastrophe. We do hope this will bring special comfort to those of you on Earth suffering the deep heartache of bereavement. The passing of time in between will appear as nothing at all one day. This, of course, applies to all bereavement for a lost loved one.

May I return your minds now to the difficult stage of the intermediary transition knowing the happy outcome at the end, which will be more fully described in our very last chapter of communication 'At the end of the Rainbow'. I wish now to take you on a short tour of our various departments within each magnificent Reception Convalescent Centre, to help you understand our specialised fields of counselling and therapeutic comfort.

Our first port of call is to enter the department of telepathic adjustment and counselling. Here, disturbed patients are slowly given advice, exercises and encouragement, to learn to differentiate their varying degrees of thought sequence. In such sudden ejection into our dimensions there had been no time to prepare their minds, which become very confused and illusory. We have to learn in Heaven to control our thought sequences continually since they are no longer strongly held back by a physical body. The new mind can run very freely and quickly, and at the same time manifest immediately what it is visualising!

For example, imagine that you build up an impression of a bowl of fruit you would like to eat. On Earth you will need to go to a shop or market to buy what was in your mind, bring it home and place the chosen varieties in a bowl. Much physical action has had to take place before that desire could be fulfilled. However, in our spiritual ethers that visualisation materialises in front of you immediately! If you want to place it on a table or on your lap, you only have to create that thought, and it happens.

When human beings are in shock from a trauma, you can now appreciate that their minds will be floating around in all directions with impressions building up around them continually, and they find themselves in a wilderness of fast moving images that never stop! The sleepful comas are indeed a temporary blessing. Upon each awakening, an experienced thought therapist purposely spotlights a healthy radiance of calm around their head to slow down the flow of images, assists each patient by explaining the various exercises necessary to control the output, and also help them to realise the difference between their own imagination, and the reality of the convalescent surroundings where they are being cared for very deeply. Slowly and surely they each come to terms with the new methods of discipline with much loving help throughout the various stages.

The other very important department during the initial recovery stages is the counselling team, who are experienced in all forms of traumatic aftermath. *(8.34pm)...(3.3.05, 8.08pm)* This particular stage of reaction upon the newcomers demands great patience and compassion on our part. Their first thoughts, as the revelation slowly sinks into their minds, are for their loved ones left behind on Earth. "How will they manage without them?" is the most common dilemma, or "How will they get on without me?" or "I want to go back at once to see them!" or "This can't happen to me, I'm going to wake up in a moment!" or "Why should I die so young!" or "I can't stay here, there is so much I wanted to do in life, I must go back!" and so on.

It breaks our hearts to witness such anguish and heartache in these tragic circumstances, but we have no choice but to apologise to each one for the unexpected outcome, which came without any due warning or mental preparation. Fate had struck them all down so suddenly with no time to face the inevitable consequences!

Our experienced counsellors and psychiatrists spend much time going over all the endless repercussions in the minds of the confused and angry patients, until a point of resignation slowly sets in.

Every luxury and comfort is offered to them from loving understanding, group therapy, soft music and healing rays, flowers, fruit, good food, pleasant walks in the beautiful grounds, and visiting ministers of every creed and denomination, who play out their sincere pastoral roll of religious counselling and spiritual upliftment. Gifts abound from relatives and friends already in our Realms and their loving presence does much to soften the blow, helping each newcomer to begin to feel a little more integrated into the new existence.

However, many tears continue to be shed over the loss of loved ones left behind on Earth. Images of their faces, the happy times together, and other events of their lives manifest like a personal video kaleidoscope, over and over again, all around them. It is as if each new soul is immersed in reliving old times, day after day, without any seeming end, until they realise that these images are purely the result of their own recall memories and not the reality.

It is at this point of bitter disappointment that the anger erupts!

"How dare God, Allah, Buddha take me away from my family and friends! I'm going back, and *no one* is going to stop me!" And we don't! A mass exodus takes place, as dozens of patients walk out of the Convalescent Centres to try to find their way back to Earth! Or so they think.

In this particular disaster aftermath they arrive on the beaches again without a boat in sight! The memory of their last moments flood back into their minds, and they automatically flee back inland in panic and terror and don't stop until they become mentally exhausted, collapsing on the ground to sleep another sleep. The sleeping souls are slowly gathered up and taken back to their rooms again in the Convalescent Centres. Upon reawakening they are all relieved to be safe from the waves.

These episodes may repeat themselves two or three times before the final reluctant acceptance dawns in their hearts, and the true radiance of Heaven begins to grow and grow like an expanding aura of brightness all around each soul body, and beyond in the beautiful environment. It is the most rewarding sight to perceive their smiling faces at last and individual resolutions to get truly well again, so they really can visit their loved ones on Earth from Heaven.

This is our third major department in the Convalescent Centres, which teaches and trains all the newcomers how to travel in thought projection to the Earth plane to indeed visit their grieving loved ones in your world. Once this has been achieved, their life in Heaven begins." *(9,12pm)*

Part Five

ATTENDING TO THE MASS OF CHILDREN

11th March 2005. 9.55pm

"Dear communicator on Earth, can you hear my voice clearly?"

"You are coming through to my mind. Thank you for being present. Are you going to dictate this chapter?"

"I shall describe only part of it, the rest will be the words from Her Royal Highness, Princess Diana, who is very devoted in Heaven to all children in need. It has become her sole occupation, and she has commanded much respect in this field. She travelled extensively on Earth, and she continues to do so in our domain, working in many international areas of the rescue work.

As a fully qualified paediatrician I have had the privilege to work alongside her in various reception zones, where children have been either very underprivileged, very badly treated, very badly abused, very badly starved and very badly diseased, as well as, very badly traumatised from the sudden shock of passing as in this Indian Ocean Zone disaster. The casualties from this enormous catastrophe were thousands upon thousands of children from all walks of life and nations. We were quite overwhelmed with the multitudes passing over from death from all the countries and islands stricken by the huge tidal waves from the under sea earthquake.

May I say here and now that the Princess was deeply grieved over such a horrendous happening on Earth? Nothing could prepare any of us in our dimensions for such a devastating natural disaster, despite the planning beforehand for every eventuality on Heaven's part. The full experience of the aftermath, as the thousands upon thousands of adults and children were rescued and received in our special Rescue Realm, was beyond our expectations. The countless moving scenes as the awakenings progressed, were heartrending to say the least, and within our own concentrated work among the little ones, many a silent tear was shed as young soul bodies were cradled in our arms, hour after hour. The dear Princess was quite beside herself with grief for them all.

As has already been explained, the Reception Centres were numerous, each with its family departments to keep loved ones together and other special children's wards with every facility of comfort and amusement. You may wonder why someone like me should need to be fully trained in child disease and deformity in the hereafter, where everyone should be perfect in mind and body. But you must appreciate that in the event of any death from Earth, the physical body would have suffered some severe condition to precipitate the passing, and we in Heaven need to understand the causes as much as your doctors and practitioners, to encourage a full psychological and emotional recovery in our dimensions.

There is always a period of adjustment to accept the inevitable change in circumstances, and another stretch of recovery to strengthen the new soul body towards perfect healing and integration into the new environment. It is rather like a baby born on Earth learning to flex its new muscles, and later trying to sit and walk. In Heaven, all ages of human beings need to practice the new thought telepathy, and overcome the lightness of their soul being in comparison to the heaviness of physicality on Earth.

Generally speaking, the children are far more accepting of the new afterlife than the adults. Upon the first awakening, the very small ones just lie in their new cots or beds just looking up at the nurses and attendants very curiously. The look of bewilderment in their eyes is very tender to our hearts as carers. A little while may pass before they begin to stir in movement. At this point they are picked up and cradled lovingly, and stroked and caressed until the warmth of our own thoughts brings a little smile to their lips.

A beautiful soft toy identical to the one they may have left behind in physical life is placed in their hands. If they had been very deprived, the sight of a new soft toy will light up their eyes and face as they clutch it tightly and hold it close to them in delight. It is a very rewarding and moving sight to see this dawn of happiness, particularly, if we are fully aware of the previous difficult background on Earth of the child.

But the very sad part is their sudden looking around for their mother or father who are absent, and the crying begins in earnest. This is the most difficult period for all ages of the children, if they are orphaned in Heaven. Grandmothers and aunts already resident in our dimensions are always on hand to bring family comfort, but there is no substitute for a parent, particularly a mother. This is where the dear Princess is so wonderfully capable of bringing a very motherly comfort to those in her charge. She spends hours consoling each one, and finds every amusement and play possible to ease their fractious moods.

She has also attended courses of child care studies at our Colleges of Learning for Rescue Work, and passed her diplomas with flying colours. She always rated her own intelligence as low, but when it comes to understanding a child's emotions she excels. When this aftermath is cleared in our Realms, she intends to apply for further training as a paediatrician herself. We hope her family on Earth will feel proud of her achievements and determination to pursue even higher qualifications. She has really found her true vocation in Heaven.

She and I were first brought together in the work during the African famine passings. I was posted there for experience following my graduation from College. The Princess was already immersed in uplifting the Earth-starved children into her welcoming arms, often two at a time, one each side of her. I arrived in the compound with this sight of her in the midst of half a dozen boys and girls pulling at her bright coloured cotton skirt. The famous Mother Teresa was also present chaperoning little ones into a long low building, where special meals were being served to them all amid much chatter and noise. The Princess caught my eye and smiled her lovely shy smile of recognition at me.

No one had explained to me beforehand that she would be present in this African compound. I had simply been told to report to this small reception complex to assist the resident paediatricians in their medical check ups. So here I was completely taken aback by her presence, and indeed that of Mother Teresa. *(10.25pm)*

12.3.05 - 3.35pm

The Princess and I had previously met for the first time at one of the Colleges of Learning. She was in her final months of examinations, and I was making a brief visit to sit in on one of the lectures of her diploma course amongst a large audience. I had come to support a close colleague, who was one of the speakers.

During the interval we were both introduced to the Princess by the head tutor. She was so lovely and completely animated by the lecture discussing childrens' emotional traumas. The three of us stood conversing on the theme very naturally as if we had known her all our lives. Her eyes met mine more than once in the course of this short social discourse, until we were called back into the auditorium for the second half of the lecture. I transported myself away in thought directly afterwards.

Several months of your Earth time passed before I found myself in this Ethiopian district to take up my first real posting. Here I was walking towards the Princess to meet her again informally, and perhaps give her a hand with the demands of the little ones surrounding her at the time. I bent down to pick up two of the African children into my own arms, and we smiled broadly at each other. I broke the ice by commenting humorously:

"We're equal now, Your Highness, two for you, and two for me!"

She giggled in amusement, and replied.

"Not for long, Doctor, if you are found talking to me, and not carrying them into the dining hall."

"In that case we shall go together and do our duty", I returned.

"With pleasure. Are you here for long?"

"I don't know yet. I've just arrived with my orders to put in a spell of help and medical examinations. For as long as it takes I imagine. And yourself, Princess Diana?"

"I don't know either - perhaps the same as you. There is constant need in this area. I'm very glad you have joined us. Please call me Diana, if we are to work together."

"Thank you. I shall feel greatly complimented."

We exchanged up to date news of events since our meeting at the College as we made our way to the long low buildings to be met by other helpers. *(3.20pm)...(6.24pm)* And so began a vocational relationship of great understanding and respect.

Our work took us to many other Realms of rescue reception wherever children were involved, including the more recent Russian massacre, until this present overwhelming catastrophe in the Indian Ocean Zone. This was to be the true test of our endurance alongside so many other helping volunteers. We were both very glad of our past experience to draw upon as we faced such a multitude of need.

So, having now given you a summary of our background work, I will hand you over to Princess Diana to carry on the description of this present scene of compassion. You will all now come to appreciate her own traumatised feelings when she passed so suddenly herself into these dimensions following that fatal car accident. She understands fully how very grieved many of the adults here are feeling, knowing they have left one or more children behind on Earth. Here is the Princess to explain in her own words that experience as she found herself in Heaven. *(6.55pm)*

*   *   *   *

"Hello! I know you're expecting me to speak over the Heavenly intercom. Are you receiving me on Earth?"

"I am indeed. Thank you so much for coming through to communicate your experiences, Your Highness"

"It is so strange hearing that title again from Earth. It was taken away from me, when I became divorced from Charles, but when I arrived here they kept calling me "Your Royal Highness", and I kept replying I wasn't anymore, until a Palace official called upon me with a scroll honouring me with the renewed title prefix. I was astonished! He was so nice and explained that Heaven was giving it back to me, because I had given heirs to the English throne, two great gifts in their eyes, and as a reward for all the charity work and devotion to duty in the public eye. So the title would remain with me in the afterlife. They see things differently here and with much more understanding.

I felt so uplifted to be appreciated when I received this official document. But before that, I had been totally distraught in the separation from my Earthly life. It is very difficult to describe without feeling all the emotion again. I felt completely cut off from the two people I loved so dearly, William and Harry, when I came round after my awakening. Like these victims in the Tsunami natural disaster my own death came 'out of the blue' unexpectedly, although I had been feeling uneasy for a while beforehand, but tried to shrug it away.

The impact, as the car crashed in the Paris tunnel, was like being punched into orbit! Within seconds I felt myself hurtling beyond the car as if into another time and space, but at the same time I was aware I was still in the tunnel. Then I blanked out! I remember being surrounded by people trying to get us out of the back seat, but I couldn't talk properly. Then I blanked out again after a searing pain in my chest. For a while I was in a twilight state of consciousness partly 'out of body' and partly aware of the physical world. Slowly my earthly body was becoming more and more uncomfortable until, finally, I was ejected fully into the after death experience.

During the interim period I had flashes of my life going before me, the very good times with William and Harry and all the appreciation from the public on my travels. These helped to draw me back into my body in the hope of recovery, but it was as if I was fighting against the tide, which was stronger than me, and in the end I was carried away. A wonderful light shone around me, and I felt gently lifted into a feeling of bliss and happiness. My father appeared and took my hand, and stood beside me for what seemed like some time. Then I fell asleep and just drifted into peace and tranquillity.

When I awoke the first time, my father was still beside me with a young man I didn't know. I was lying on a very beautiful couch surrounded by masses of flowers. The perfumes were unbelievable. My first thoughts were that I must be recovering after all. But my father, catching my thoughts, just said,

"It's all over Diana, it's all over!"

I didn't know what he meant until a lovely nurse came to the side of the couch and said, "Your Royal Highness, you are in Heaven now!"

"Your Royal Highness" sounded so strange to me at the time. The fact that she gave me the title at all helped me to realise something was different. My father then turned to me saying:

"I want you to meet John, your elder brother. He died soon after he was born."

John came forward to hold my hand as I looked up at him in surprise!

"Dear Diana, we meet for the first time," he spoke quietly to me. "You have suffered so much. I will help you all I can to adjust to this new life, and we will get to know each other.

I could hardly take it all in after so much sudden change.

"Thank you, John. . ." was all I could reply as I drifted back to sleep again.

It took several awakenings before the full truth dawned in my mind and heart. Then the flood gates opened! I cried and cried and cried! I couldn't stop! Everything about my life hit me, and hit me! Everything I had bottled up came to the surface and burst out! This change had happened so suddenly! Why? Why? Why? Just when life seemed to be opening up for me, and then the door was slammed shut!

And Dodi, what had happened to him? In my twilight consciousness in the car, I had sensed he had passed out completely, but I was too helpless myself to do anything for him! Where was he now? Why were we not together? In death we were separated. But not for too long.

He was recovering like me from the huge shock of the crash. His own passing had been instant. He was comatosed for quite a while. It actually took him longer to come to the full realisation of the outcome. *(8.33pm)* Meantime, my own grief at being parted from my beloved boys, William and Harry was continuous. Little could comfort me from the terrible separation while they were both young. How could I survive without them, and how would they cope without my loving support? *(8.44pm)*

19.3.05 - 3.55pm

In the middle of my grief, the Lord visited me in the lovely private recovery villa to bring his sincere commiserations. He sat down beside me like a 'Dutch Uncle' and held my hand in comfort. He has a very kind manner.

"My dearest Princess Diana, my heart reaches out to you so deeply, and so do the people of Britain in every far corner. You may well be feeling their deep shock and distress of your sudden passing, alongside your own. Reports are coming to us of a mass outbreak of grief for your earthly departure. Thousands are already laying flowers outside the gates of Kensington Palace in your loving memory. I do hope this moving spectacle will bring you a little consolation, and the knowledge that the British public are with you very much in thought."

This was the first news I had been given from back home in the physical world. I was astonished! When I was later invited into the Summerland Palace gardens a day or so your time before my funeral on Earth, I stood amazed at the incredible collection of flowers, bouquets and posies laid out as far as the eye could see in those extensive grounds in Heaven. One of the officials escorted me round many of the areas to read some of the messages. It took a long time just viewing one small area of the floral tributes. The Palace official explained that every bloom gathered in my memory on Earth had been transposed in thought to this Heavenly Realm for me to see, and every message recorded upon the ethers and reproduced attached to the appropriate bouquet. My tears flowed continuously in home sickness as I wandered through this enormous display of flowers and emotional notes.

I returned to my convalescent villa with my new lady-in-waiting feeling moved beyond any words could ever describe. May I take this opportunity to thank you all, wherever you may be, for this incredible personal tribute not only from Britain, but from many other nations around the world. Thank you with all my heart, so very much. It did uplift me, and helped me to feel so appreciated from Earth.

The next step in this new existence was to attend my own funeral, which I knew would be emotionally very difficult. I was prepared a day beforehand by the Lord explaining the procedure on Earth, and the part I was to take as an invisible visitor upon the scene. I was to ride in an open carriage beside my father, which was to travel behind the funeral gun carriage and its escort on the day. At St James' Palace, I would disembark with my father to join my new brother and others to walk behind my brother Charles, William and Harry, Prince Charles and the Duke of Edinburgh, to Westminster Cathedral.

But before the day dawned, the news of Mother Teresa's passing was brought to me. She was awakening in a private chapel room in the Summerland Palace, where I was invited to greet her with the Lord. We sat either side of her couch, which was also surrounded by flowers and many candles lit in the background. Her face was very serene, and as she opened her eyes to see the Lord looking down at her and then me, she just said in her thoughts:

"I'm in Heaven, aren't I?" and smiled.

We remained talking with her for a short while before departing as she closed her eyes to sleep again.

By now, Dodi had come round several times during his soul sleeps and asked after me. He was in a private ward of a Convalescent Reception Centre not far away. I was taken to see him by a Palace official and my personal lady-in-waiting.

He was very pleased to see me as I sat down beside him. We held hands in mutual commiseration, the tears pouring down both our cheeks as the memories of our recent happy times together on Earth, flooded into our thoughts. He was very upset, too, that he had died young. What was he going to do now, he questioned to me? Everything in his life had been left behind except me, and even I was separated from him. My royal standing had been given back, which might create a division between us. It may not be appropriate to carry on as before in these new circumstances.

We must help each other and remain good friends, I assured him, as the nurse came back to take him to a counselling session, and usher me out too.

"The dear Princess is not strong herself yet, Sir. You have left behind a whole way of life, and she has left behind two much beloved sons. There are great losses for both of you, but Heaven's healing love will help you each to find strength and happiness again. She faces visiting her own funeral tomorrow, a very public and national affair. You will do her great good by supporting her like her father and brother, among others."

Dodi fell silent for a few moments, and then answered with a smile.

"It will be my honour to be among the party to support her."

(5.13pm)

1.4.05 - 9.05pm

I'm not going to dwell too much on the funeral, because I want you all to realise I am alive and well in another unseen world. But at the same time I want to express my very sincere appreciation of the incredible loyalty and devotion you all showed in such emotion towards my departure from my Earth life, before and during my funeral. I felt the loss too very deeply, not only from being apart from my boys, but also from the public support given to me so spontaneously during my physical life as a Royal, and at the end.

I was completely overwhelmed as I was vibrationally lowered into the earthly vibrations and saw for myself the thousands of people lining the streets along the route of the funeral procession to Westminster Abbey. I was totally unprepared for such a moving demonstration of love and respect.

As the gun carriage emerged from Kensington Palace, my father and I were seated in an open carriage behind it, quite invisible to your eyes. But we were able to see you all quite clearly, a privilege given to me for the occasion. Tears were rolling down my cheeks as we passed you all on either side of the streets. Driving alongside Buckingham Palace again was so strange, and seeing the flag at half mast.

When we came to St James' Palace we disembarked to walk behind my brother, William and Harry, Charles and his father. At the sight of my sons I broke down completely and held onto my father on one side and my brother John on the other, while Heaven gave me healing strength. Dodi walked behind with his hand on my shoulder for comfort too. The healing radiance helped me to calm down a little, and a soft mist enveloped me as we continued walking in silence. It slowly cleared for me to see my sons again.

When we came to the cathedral we were ahead of the walking party so I was able to turn to see William and Harry more face to face as they arrived at the entrance. Inside, I was escorted up the aisle with my father, brother and Dodi to the chancel to view the whole funeral service. Mother Teresa joined our group, and sat beside me holding my hand throughout. I was given a wonderful view of my beloved sons, a mixture of happiness and heartbreak for me. I was very proud of how well they stood up to the occasion. As my brother Charles gave his speech the emotion welled up inside me so much. Seeing members of my own family was very moving too, and I have also missed them very much.

The one thing that Heaven blurred completely during the funeral was the coffin. It was quite extraordinary seeing an empty space where it should have been, so for me it was just like being present at a memorial service. I was told afterwards that a simple wreath of white roses had been placed on top from William and Harry. The beautiful arrangement was handed to me in the evening at the villa with the note attached to it. I have treasured it ever since. The everlasting roses go with me everywhere I travel, where I stay for long periods for the rescue work, and the card and words are in a little gold frame by my bed.

May I take this opportunity to say hello to dear William and Harry and let them know Mummy is with them so often in thought, and continues to surround them in her love and encouragement as much as possible. I miss you both so, so much, and always will. But I am able to watch over your lives from time to time, and am given glimpses of your futures, which help me to guide you both in the best way I can. Heaven gives me this special compensation as she does for all parents in Spirit separated from young children on Earth.

When the funeral service was over, I found myself uplifted back into the higher Realms, until a later glimpse was given to me of the island resting place at Althorp.

Dodi and I met frequently during our recoveries to talk and go over our lives, which came to us in detail as we were each given our Life Reviews to analyse our gains and losses, and how well we had lived our lives generally. We compared notes with each other, and discussed how we were going to move forward in this new life.

He was given the opportunity to meet up with new acquaintances in the Spirit world, and to feel his way into a new area of film making. I was later offered the chance to help Mother Teresa with many children passing into Heaven from starvation, cruelty, deprivation and so on. Our paths separated for a while to test our feelings for each other. We both needed to pursue what was closest to our hearts, and meet up every so often to talk it all over.

The sudden car accident in Paris had been so traumatic that it had somehow stopped us both in our tracks very hard and abruptly, and frightened us about coming together again. We became more like brother and sister in the end, someone to talk to as we both struggled to find our feet in this new situation and to share the heartaches. The young driver killed in the accident too was very demented for a while. Dodi took him under his wing, and helped him as much as he could. *(10.37pm)*

6.4.05 - 9.55pm

My work among the heavenly children has totally absorbed my mind and helped me to realise how lucky I was on Earth. Even though I am now cut off from my beloved sons, William and Harry, and shed a million tears in my grief from the separation, I realise life does go on for us all whether 'up here' or 'down there'. I know one day we will be reunited together again, and we will have so much to talk about when that future comes. Meantime, I have been given such wonderful opportunities to come to understand the minds and emotions of the boys and girls of all ages, who have passed over from death into Heaven. My new brother John was true to his promise, as he escorted me on many occasions to visit individual children and childrens' centres.

I want you to know that I have met many of the children, who died during my physical life, who I had visited in hospital or in their homes on Earth. It was heartbreaking at the time, but when I saw them again in these Realms quite well and happy after their ordeals, I was quite overcome. It was like seeing a happy ending and their life going on in a more beautiful environment. The sadness was that they were separated from their families like me, but everyone is so helpful and supportive towards bringing happiness in this new lease of life for all newcomers.

Children who have been handicapped from birth on Earth receive very special attention in Heaven. My first period of care was to be with the previously blind, deaf and disabled from Earth. They wake up in these Realms being able to see and hear for the first time, but they have to learn about what they see and hear! If you have never seen a tree or a house in your physical life, when you see them in Spirit it is like going to a foreign land not knowing what they are. It's like starting at the beginning again, so we point out various objects and name them in words to help them learn. The same is for the deaf children. They had been used to seeing and understanding sign language, now they could hear words, but we would have to spell them out in sign language and writing to help them understand what they were listening to. Just as colour and shapes fascinated the previously blind children, music and singing brought wonderful smiles to the previously deaf. In Heaven, we were forever watching miracles as these youngsters began to live a new life with all their faculties and senses.

Watching the disabled learn to stand, the Down's Syndrome start to think clearly and normally, and those with the many other forms of handicaps become whole and normal was the tonic and upliftment I needed to heal my own heartbreak. In their joy and happiness becoming perfect, many would fling their arms round us to show how excited they were to become quite normal, a new and wonderful experience for them all. Whatever they had lost on Earth they gained in Heaven. I want to bring this hope to all the parents and families in physical life, who may have lost their children with handicaps or deformities. I want you to know that one day you will see them again, when your time comes to pass into Heaven, and you will cry with joy to see them so well and normal.

I travelled to many different areas in our Spirit Summerlands with John to visit various Reception Centres catering for children and young people, to experience their awakenings in the afterlife and the amazing transformations. I still find it hard to believe, and every new miracle brings tears to my eyes. But most of all, the little babies developed from all forms of miscarriages are unbelievable. These very tiny beginnings from physical life are incubated to the full term of birth, at which point they are taken out of the protective cocoon and laid in a normal cradle. They do not have the trauma of birth, and are allocated a relative or foster mother to care for them, like a formal adoption. One day they will be reunited with their true parents.

The first incubating unit I visited showed me all the various stages of the babies' developments. When we came to the full term babies in cradles, one of the nurses bent down and picked up a beautiful baby boy and laid him in my arms. He was so lovely.

"Would you like to be mother to this one, Your Highness?" she asked me smiling broadly.

I was so taken aback I couldn't answer straight away. The tears just rolled down my face as I gazed adoringly at his little face.

"We know how much you miss your boys on Earth and always will, but the Lord asked us to offer you a baby to look after, or an older child, as our gift for all the work you did for children on Earth. If you get on well, we may find another to keep this one company, so you can feel more of a family."

I walked out of that unit with a new son in my arms, and when he began toddling, I was given a baby girl. A new experience for me!

15.4.05 - 9.05pm

My new life in Heaven took on a happier period of purpose and care. James, Sarah and I lived together with my father in a lovely house in the parkland of the Summerland Palace, a government and administration centre. We were all learning together, and Dodi was a frequent visitor among others. He was building a new life in filming and was always full of all the latest developments on location, and the spirit technology he was learning in this renewed vocation.

When my two adopted children were three and two years old, Mother Teresa came to see me, as she did from time to time, and described her latest work with the African children and mothers, who were passing over from starvation and neglect. My heart reached out to them all, and I began to yearn to help and make myself more useful. I had been given a time of peace to settle down in Heaven with my new family, but now I felt I must take on some work in service to pay a little back for all I had been given.

"I have spoken to the Lord on your behalf," Mother Teresa told me at the end of her conversation. "He agreed with me that you might like to spread your wings and see for yourself some of the wonderful work being carried out for these unfortunate victims, and learn more of Heaven's ways. You could bring your new children with you, and if you felt happy to give some help, the Lord would recommend you to a college to gain some special training. You've always loved children, so we felt this work might appeal to you."

How could I refuse? A few weeks later, I travelled with father, John, nanny and children to the area where Mother Teresa was working, and stayed a little longer than originally planned. It was as she suggested very much my field of care, and I learnt so much about Heaven's rescue work, first hand. James and Sarah were wonderful allies with me, and made many new friends.

When we returned to our home, I was offered private study papers, and frequent weekend seminars at college. It was at one of these sessions that I first met Richard, and months later saw him again, as he has already explained, at the African compound and Reception Centre. Another phase in both our lives opened up. I felt so at home with him, shared the same devotion to the children, and we seemed to work so well together. We shared other assignments in the work.

James and Sarah were now going to school and learning very quickly under a lovely teacher. I was often allowed in class to watch and help the slower ones. Thought here is very fast, and minds are clear to understand, but even here each child learns at their own pace. It was all new and fascinating to me, and helped me so much to appreciate the needs of all children passing over in difficult circumstances or tragedies.

When the pending Ocean Zone Earthquake was announced, long before it was due to happen on Earth, Richard and I offered our services, straight away. My children were old enough now to stay behind and carry on at school without me. My father and nanny were there to look after them.

Richard and I travelled together with a large group of trained child carers and paediatricians to Thailand, where we were booked in at one of the special childcare Reception Centres, and prepared ourselves for the onslaught. The reality was enormous! Nothing could have prepared us for what lay ahead. The mass of children passing over was beyond anything any of us had imagined, and the time it took for the initial awakenings to settle down, plus the massive rehabilitation afterwards, seemed endless! Once we got fully underway there was hardly time to take a breath. *(10.10pm)*

24.4.05 - 3.47pm

Dodi was also present in the Rescue Realm, offering consulation to many of the casualties, while visiting the wards in the Reception Convalescent Centres. He and his young lady assistant from the East were also filming, with a large crew, the many moving developments throughout the rescue and recovery operation, to illustrate this very valuable heavenly work for future volunteers. We met up with them on several occasions.

Meanwhile, as each new contingent of children arrived at our particular Reception Centre, I stood by with other carers in the admission hall to greet each one, and to comfort them in their bewilderment after their first awakenings. Some would be brought in on trolleys, and others were carried in by nurses and orderlies.

Many of them would be crying, or just whimpering quietly. I would walk by the trolleys and talk to the children being wheeled in towards an examination cubicle, where Richard would be waiting to examine each one in our charge, to discern their past physical health.

The soul body is a complete replica of the earthly counterpart, and from the time of passing over at death it emits shadows and dark spots, which indicate past weaknesses of ill health. Once these have been identified, we can set a programme of full recovery for each individual. In the case of the Tsunami disaster, the greatest percentages of deaths were from drowning, and therefore the lungs would have been badly affected.

Here is a scene to illustrate our initial work as the children of all ages are passed through our hands.

A little girl is prostrate on a trolley and looking at me with such fear in her eyes. I take her hand in mine and smile back as kindly as I can. She responds by calming down and looking less anxious as she gazes intently back at me.

"We are here to keep you safe and make you happy again", I tell her, "We are taking you to see a doctor who will help you to feel better." Her eyes plead at me in fear again. "I will stay by your side all the time. He is very kind and understanding". She grips my hand very hard, and I smile down at her in great love knowing what she has gone through. It is all I can do to control my own tears in the tragedy of it all.

We enter the cubicle where Richard works and has examined countless others before this little girl, and she begins to cry in earnest!

"Diana, can you lift her into your arms for a while to calm her down. I will take some vibrational readings at the same time, which she will not notice at all". I do as Richard asks, and between us the task is carried out, and the sobbing subsides as the little girl relaxes in my arms. I give her a hug and a kiss to reassure her, and pull a soft toy out of our box to give to her. She clasps it to herself, and I receive her first smile! I lay her on the trolley and escort her with the orderly to a children's ward.

I then go back to collect and comfort the next child for Richard, who fills in the details of each patient in between time. This procedure is repeated hundreds and thousands of times, day after day, from babies to early teenagers, and attended to by the hundreds and thousands of trained staff volunteering their services in every other childcare Reception Centre, as well as our own.

The next stage is visiting them in the wards and trying to pacify their fear and shock at the sudden change. We make this new existence as near to Earth in familiarity as possible with pictures on the walls, toys, books and story telling. When they are more recovered we organise games and little lessons of thought activities, helping them to understand their new environment and how it differs from physical life. We get them to dress up in characters from the stories we tell, by helping them to create their costumes or hats from visual creativity. They all enjoy this very much, and we all have many laughs when it doesn't quite work out as expected, so they also enjoy the unexpected funny surprises!

If they have been separated from their parents or family members, who are still alive on Earth, their sadness lasts quite a while, just as the bereavement is felt by those left behind in your world. Other relatives in Heaven try to take their place and care for them with love in our dimensions. There is always someone, or a group to foster them in our Realms, where they will grow up and go to school as on Earth. The children generally cope very much better than the adults in these circumstances, but it is still a big challenge for their young minds.

As Richard and I worked with all those in our charge we gained so much more experience. The sheer volume of numbers was overwhelming, but as we got to know many of them personally over the weeks in your time during the recovery period, we came to understand the characteristics and customs of many nationalities. We realised how much we now felt at home with children from all over the world during this huge avalanche of casualties. The task of rehabilitation was to carry on for some months, and we felt strongly we would like to continue with the work in this area of Thailand and all the neighbouring countries and Islands. We offered our services to the authorities, which were gratefully accepted. *(9.15pm)*

Part Six

PLANNING THE FUTURE AND VISITING EARTH

29th May 2005. 9.30pm

"May I introduce myself?"

"Please do. I'm hearing a female voice."

"I am one of many ladies and gentleman that serve in the Rehabilitation Centres set up for this Tsunami catastrophe. We are here to interview the countless casualties from Earth, whatever their age from physical life, and help them create a new future for themselves in our many dimensions. Once an immediate plan for the near future has been settled upon, the tormented new souls begin to enjoy greater calm and positive thought in Heaven. When the Reception Centres send us the reports of their change in attitudes and acceptance of their new existence in our domains, we are then called upon to make visits to the wards to access the needs and desires of each individual in our care for their rehabilitation.

Many will have been separated from their families on Earth, and many will be disturbed that they have left aspects of their life behind that are unfinished or unresolved. They cannot go back to put it all in order as they wish, and this can bring much distress to their hearts and minds. Such sudden and immediate transition into our Realms left no time at all to attend to such matters.

Therefore our departments of 'Unfinished Business' are amongst the first they all wish to visit, where our experts in these fields of counselling talk over all their anxieties, and suggest how they can help to remedy the situations by thought infiltration to those near and dear to them left behind in physical life. This in itself entails special training to accomplish these ends, and guide each man and woman towards a new peace of mind in the happier outcomes.

Meantime, past relatives visit the new souls regularly in the Reception Centres, and slowly the new family members and long settled loved ones in our Realms exchange news, and get to know each other. Some may have never met each other before, so it is a case of being introduced to virtual strangers. The past relatives can do a lot to help the newcomers for us by chatting about their own lives and experiences in Heaven, and often offering to take them under their wings by inviting them to their own abodes, as an initial taste of their new life beyond the Reception Centres.

But first and foremost, there are many papers to be filled in as on Earth, such as forms of identification, details of past work, family and experiences from physical life, and possible desires of new vocations and communal grouping. Every nation and culture is represented in our dimensions, and also every geographical country.

Some individuals may have been deeply deprived on Earth, and so we endeavour to fulfil many lost needs or secret ambitions that were thwarted in their past life, due to conflicting attitudes or very limiting situations. Every possible blessing is given to all the victims from this Indian Ocean Zone disaster, since their lives were sacrificed and terminated so traumatically and unexpectedly. It is as if Heaven waves a magic wand and grants every possible lost opportunity to each and every one of the Earth casualties, as a fulfilling compensation for the great loss of their lives so suddenly.

Perhaps the greatest prize of all is the regaining of a youthful appearance for those who were mature in years prior to death.

Their delight to find themselves slowly gaining long forgotten prime years of their thirties brings untold upliftment to their hearts. Their skin smoothes out from wrinkles, their figures take on perfect proportions, and minds become alert and fully active once more.

The young ones mature very much slower than on Earth, in as much as the full flowering into adulthood is maintained at the correct stage of development without any deviation, either youger or older as on Earth. But once they reach their peak of development, they remain in youthful looks and never grow old. However, they need to gain much in wisdom and understanding within these domains. *(10.35pm)*

7.6.05 - 8.35pm

From the nursery years to young adulthood we provide all the basic education they could wish for in knowledge and information within a variety of curriculums, plus a strong influence upon human virtues and community social services. Tolerance, humility, selflessness, patience and diligence begin at the earliest ages, and continue in discipline long into adulthood. All the general subjects are multi-dimensional in our Realms, owing to the fact that the thought sequences of every developing young soul is capable of creating mind visions instantaneously from the information given at each lesson.

For example, a history lesson on the ancient Greeks can produce a video form of collective thought production with encouragement from the teacher, to allow the whole class to enjoy a first hand experience of that long lost era. Girls and boys will feel themselves dressed as Greeks, feel themselves walking the streets together or roaming the landscape, entering the buildings or meeting ancient Greeks in their everyday lives in a form of dream sequence that is real and educational. Geography would be the same with visits to different countries or continents. Languages would also come into this latter category.

Story telling would produce reality 'dream videos' from

the creative imaginations, and above all, artistic pastimes would bring endless designs and permutations from each individual pupil as they mould their thoughts into materialisations. It is far more than just reading, writing and practical experiments, it is all these activities alongside further three-dimensional and time-dimensional realities, rather like being within and part of a film or video sequence.

All school and college studies are very happy and entertaining; Even tiny tots, however limited their minds may be, delight in their fairy stories coming to life, their soft toys animating before their eyes from their own thought longings, and their rides on hobby horses, toy cars, and four wheeled 'push alongs' turn into real journeys of their little imaginations. They concentrate on their pastimes for hours, and link into the day dreams of their close companions. Into an empty cardboard box a host of objects and toys of their own invention can materialise like a fairy waving a magic wand!

The mature adults can continue with the work or hobbies they enjoyed the most on Earth, ranging from the indoors to the outdoors. When they leave the Reception Centres, we encourage them to enjoy a well deserved holiday of their own choice first. This may take the form of a long stay with a lost relative or friend already existing in our dimensions; or perhaps a time to explore a new environment of their former domain on Earth; or indeed travel to somewhere completely new they had always dreamed of going to one day. The casualties from this particular catastrophe, and indeed other disasters, will be offered every possible opportunity to enjoy their first few months, your time, in Heaven to overcome their frustrations or heartbreak at leaving their physical lives so dramatically. The healing balm of new horizons is indeed the joy we seek to bring them in the initial stages of their new existence.

Some souls may decide right at the beginning what they wish to do after their vacationary period in the way of continued work or profession as on Earth, new college training or apprenticeships, or seek to join our community of welfare services throughout the many Realms and Spheres. The choice is endless and echoes every possible employment as in physical life, but on much higher wavelengths.

For instance, transport remains as remembered on Earth, but is far smoother and more finely powered. Our helicopter aircraft in Part 2 is a good example. Engines are silent, 'fuel' is recycled, and internal controls are very advanced and efficient in thought wavelengths. Any past pilot from physical life will need to take on further training to understand the more advanced heavenly technology of thought manipulation. Every career or vocation in our dimensions of Spirit will require new education and aptitudes to understand the higher frequencies. *(9.47pm)*

9.6.05 - 8.35pm

Our Halls of Learning, as already known among Spirit communicating circles, offer wide curriculums of adult education, from short day talks and lectures, to week-long seminars and progressively longer periods of learning. Those who have suffered little education on Earth can start at the beginning and follow through to advanced studies. No-one is allowed to feel inadequate in their understanding, but simply encouraged in every way at their own pace to make up all they may have lost in physical life. Heaven is here to provide the very best in educational upliftment for all concerned at whatever stage or need, whether elementary, intermediate or advanced. Many who have had a yen to learn a particular subject, craft or intellect, but were never able to follow it through on Earth due to many limiting reasons, can fulfil their dream in great personal joy.

Those who are quite undecided as to what they wish to do or learn can wander through our special Exhibition Halls of many stalls, departments, film and lecture halls to ascertain a particular interest that may fire their imagination. These huge buildings promote every possible attraction towards new careers, vocations and pastimes. Souls rarely visit such wonderful arenas of illustrative information without returning with great enthusiasm for several aspects of future employment that has captivated their minds.

Several huge Exhibition Halls were built and set up for this Tsunami disaster Rescue Realm to inspire hearts and minds towards their futures. Schools, colleges and universities also offered wonderful open days and weeks for inspection with a taste of all that is on their timetables, plus personal interviews with tutors and professors. Booklets and brochures were available to take back to Reception Centres, and all the 'world wide web' sites that so many of you are familiar with on Earth are here in special computer rooms with the highest and fastest mind research technology imaginable. All newcomers need to train and adjust to these alone.

Finally, after much investigation and pleasurable visits to various promotional buildings for information, the new souls are invited to the Rehabilitation Centre to talk it all through with those of us on hand to guide and advise the way ahead. New homes, new surroundings, new interests, past experience, personal desires all need to be taken into consideration. This can sometimes be quite simple, but more often quite complicated matching up all the various aspects. Applications, practical feasibilities, and possible availabilities must all be taken into account very deeply. All these new souls tragically aborted from physical life into our Heavenly Realms require much adjustment to accept their new existence, and are given loving patience and understanding on our part. Some may settle fairly quickly, whilst others may take a long time to come to terms with the new situation.

Once we can establish the first stage of each soul's future, we begin to plan the next period of rehabilitation, and so on. Above all, we seek to make it all as relaxing and as pleasurable as possible, and prepare their voyage of discovery with future happiness in mind.

We must deal with many cultures and nationalities, as well as many likely geographical locations. Immigration and emigration may be high priorities for many catastrophe victims, especially those residing in the stricken areas. The fear and terror may precipitate the desire for a completely new country and lifestyle. We foster no restrictions in such a severe catastrophe as in the Indian Ocean Zone earthquake. All are free to choose a new destination, or return to their original habitat, which is reflected in our 'Summerlands' very closely in landscape and community culture. However, we pride ourselves that our many improvements in architecture, town and city planning, environmental perfection and beauty, bring many gasps of surprise and admiration from the newcomers, and more importantly from those who feel they have returned 'home'.

But for every casualty from the disaster passing from death into our dimensions, 'home' may still be on Earth in their hearts and minds. Very few will begin to really settle until they have made at least one visit back to Earth. They long so much to see loved ones again, and find out how they are coping without them.

Our Recovery Realm contains wonderful healing vibrations within its atmosphere, which provide a protecting safety net for the thousands of new souls within its confines. When they are sufficiently recovered and settled, it allows them a gentle freedom to explore other frequencies. If they were to descend in thought too soon to the denser, mental environment of Earth, they would be pulled down into a feeling of deep depression, and may find it harder to rise up and come back into the comfort of our domains. For this reason, we keep them as long as possible in the recovery area to prepare them fully in thought sequence and discipline, before taking this important maiden voyage to visit their relatives and friends left behind in physical life. *(9.53pm)*
13.6.05 - 10.40pm

Love is the 'bridge' between Heaven and Earth. It is love, and love alone, which draws the minds and hearts of our new souls towards their loved ones still in physical life, and it is these latter loved ones whose mind and hearts have been dwelling deeply upon those they have lost in their grief and heartache. Their longing for those lost beyond death creates a link for those also trying to come to terms with the sudden separation now in our Realms of Heaven.

During the initial awakenings already described, and the later confusion of the new surroundings, many of our new souls see many glimpses of their past loved ones very clearly during dream states and telepathic wanderings. They reach out for them, but like many near death experiences from Earth, there is an invisible barrier that gently separates them through which they cannot pass, and so they simply gaze in wonder until the vision fades.

Many recount these experiences to their nurses, orderlies and counsellors in our Reception Realms, and they are all encouraged to enjoy the sight of past family and friends in these unexpected mental sequences. These fleeting visions build up in thought as idealised longings, and help to bring comfort to their hearts. But as time progresses these materialised imaginings are no longer enough to appease their feeling of home sickness for their family and friends on Earth. They want to see for themselves how they truly are, and how they may be coping without their presence in physical life beside them.

We try hard to reassure them that although the heavy cloud of bereavement hangs over their loved ones back home, the higher powers of light and angelic protection will ultimately guide them back to balance and harmony in their lives on Earth once more, however long it may take. This will depend entirely upon each individual capacity to accept and come to terms with the tragic loss. Every beauty and comfort will be brought back into their lives, slowly and steadily until a point is reached, when they can move forward with their destinies in more strength and resolve.

While our souls are being advised to plan their futures ahead in our dimensions, many lovely guides of all nationalities, who shadowed every victim during their earthly existence, infiltrate into the Recovery Realm to act as escorts for their prodigies on the earthly expeditions. Completely unknown to most of the Tsunami casualties, these dedicated and trained souls are at last introduced to them, and yet another stage of awakening takes place.

The surprise and wonder to discover that each individual has indeed a devoted guardian angel, brings a new dimension of upliftment and deep appreciation of God's love and protection. We cannot underestimate to you all still on Earth, that more than one unseen helper is guiding you and sustaining you during the very difficult times in life, and endeavouring to lead you to all the spiritual truths and deeper understanding of universal love. Your pilgrimage may take many twists and turns, but ultimately all your experiences will mould every facet of each new awareness into a clear and coherent purpose towards greater enlightenment and wisdom. *(10.50pm)*

16.6.05 - 3.55pm

As the guides assemble slowly and unobtrusively, relatives already residing in our Realms take the cue to invite their kith and kin among the new souls, to practice visualising their loved ones on Earth time after time, until each newcomer is confident of their skill and successfully build up materialised images long enough to sustain each vision for a period of time. Once this first stage has been established, the 'bridge of love' will begin to open up the 'divide' between Heaven and Earth by blending the two varying vibration wavelengths, and heightening the energies and protection for the journey down the frequencies to visit the physical plane.

It is at this point of the preparation that the higher guides and guardian angels bring their presence alongside each individual soul seeking to visit loved ones on Earth. Light and radiance is drawn from our highest Spheres to surround all the travellers, who will descend in groups as further safety and mutual comfort.

The earthly vibrations will feel heavy and dense as the chosen parties slowly find themselves closer and closer to physical life. When they finally reach the particular geographical area through concentrated thought direction on the part of the guides, the new heavenly souls must then begin to build up the images of their dear ones left behind on Earth, and believe themselves very close in proximity.

Suddenly, without warning they are instantly walking, standing or sitting near their loved ones in their homes, work or community, just as they remember these locations prior to death. But they are, of course, invisible and can no longer talk to them physically. However, their presence can often be felt quite strongly, as has been reported countless times from many who have lost loved ones in every circumstance of death. It is by no means uncommon for a spirit to be 'seen' at some point in the first few months following their passing.

For our new souls taking this maiden voyage it can be a very emotional experience, in the same way that those on Earth can feel very moved during a private sitting with a medium, who demonstrates distinctive evidence of continued existence of their lost loved ones in the afterlife. But unlike the case of our souls, the link from Earth will be very transitory, whereas from the heavenly vantage point our souls can remain with those left behind in physical life for as long as the energies allow them to stay. Time is manoeuvrable in the Spirit world, but as our new souls focus their minds within the earthly vibrations and feel the reality of their very light subtle bodies in comparison to the physicality of those they are visiting, they become more attuned to your world and its time.

As they draw very close to loved ones left behind on Earth, they can detect their emotions and feelings, and monitor any inner unhappiness. Each soul is advised beforehand to send out as much loving thought and cheerfulness as possible to bring them comfort. They will even put their invisible arms round their shoulders, or stretch out an invisible hand to caress their brow. Perhaps just living a day or so around their physical life helps them to feel they are still caring for them, albeit in thought only, and at the same time receiving a good idea of how they are coping without them.

This initial visitation may be the first of many as the months and years progress until such time as new life is restored on both sides, and each party, whether in Heaven or left behind on Earth, can move forward in their separate lives again in greater strength and optimism for the future. They will ultimately meet up one day in very joyful reunion in Heaven." *(4.45pm)*

Part Seven

'AT THE END OF THE RAINBOW'

17th June 2005. 9.07pm

"My dearest lady, our deepest peace be with you. Can you hear me clearly?

"I can indeed, thank you, and I am happy to transcribe this part from you, dear Brother."

"May I first take this opportunity to thank you for your dedicated endeavour to promote this documentary sequel for your earthly world. Many of the casualties from the Indian Ocean Zone catastrophe await in great expectation of reaching the minds of their lost loved ones left behind in physical life through this testimony, and in so doing, bring them consolation that they are indeed 'alive and well' in our dimensions. Although they may have suffered emotionally in confusion, grief and anger for a while in this lower Heaven as they awoke to the reality of their very sudden and unexpected transition, nevertheless, the final adjustment to the new consciousness is now rising into joy and happiness within the radiant surroundings, and with every new opportunity they are being offered for the future.

I myself have sojourned in the heavenly dimensions for numerous centuries, and during that extensive time, as on Earth, I have served humanity in the many different Spheres. 'In my Father's

House are many Mansions' is a very true saying, and each so called 'Mansion' or Realm vibrates at varying thought frequencies in graded degrees upwards to the very High Realms of Light.

When I first passed into the afterlife, I remained close to the earthly vibrations for some while in order to uplift souls from traumatic deaths. The many centuries have brought untold wars, battles, plagues, torture and martyrdoms to name but a few, and like this particular natural disaster, as indeed like every other natural disaster, each has been attended to very deeply by our Spirit domains. We will continue to do so while, sadly, there is a need.

Gradually, I moved up the levels of the Spheres, experiencing and learning many lessons of understanding, until I finally reached the Realms of Light, where I remained as a Governor for a considerable period.

The beauty of the landscape is indescribable, the grace of the architecture beyond compare, and the loving tolerance and unity of the inhabitants, whether socially high or low in the communities, is the true Heaven. As the radiant environment shines its perfection upon the people, so they in turn reflect their own loving light back to enhance the overall beauty and atmosphere.

However, many of these very evolved and perfected souls sacrifice this joy and happiness to travel down the Spheres, from time to time, with the sincere purpose of uplifting the minds, hearts and attitudes of the lower levels towards a truer perspective of love and understanding. I have been no exception, and have gained a broader, more panoramic view of every aspect of life in the process. It is very necessary for those of us fortunate enough to reside in the Realms of Light, to 'take time out', as you might say, and gain further knowledge and experience of the lower levels, to ascertain the strengths and weaknesses of the continuing evolvement of all souls. Otherwise, we become so imbued with the enfoldment of all the intense love, light and beauty, that we are in danger of being enclosed in an ivory tower.

The great varieties of life or existence on all dimensions is a diversity of endless fascination, whether good or bad, and our full experience of the overall picture increases the continuing depth of our understanding, which is greatly needed in all areas of human and other creature needs.

Returning to the Tsunami rescue and recovery work, experienced Brothers and Sisters from every high level in Heaven, descended the Spheres to be on hand, and act as overseers in every department of the general awakening and rehabilitation. They mingle very humbly and diligently among all the helpers, bringing gentleness, patience, understanding, and above all, great human compassion.

After reading through the previous parts of this documentary, you will now be reasonably aware of the many problems that had to be overcome, and the enormous volume of support needed to see through the many stages of acceptance for the incoming souls from the very traumatic catastrophe of their deaths. During their periods of mental disturbance, the deep understanding of the very experienced Brothers and Sisters of Light is greatly appreciated by the many helpers learning to cope with it all. *(10.20pm)*

29.6.05 - 2.58pm

Long before this natural disaster took place, an incredible outpouring of radiance drifted down the many vibrational layers from the Highest Realms of Light. It continued, and it continued, day and night, for days and weeks, slowly permeating every square inch of the potential areas likely to be stricken by the terrible under water earthquake and the lethal tidal waves rising up in its wake.

Once those regions had been saturated with this very gentle power of ultimate healing energy, the world in general was illuminated with many other outpourings of heavenly radiance according to the personal need, whether individual, family group or community, which were to be deeply involved in the earthly emergency services and aid, and the thousands of relatives likely to be deeply mourning their dead in the final outcome.

Alongside the preparational radiance descending to Earth were countless angelic beings taking up their positions in every far corner of the Indian Ocean Zone. Their own strength of presence stood like beacons of fortitude before and during the onslaught, and their further healing rays enfolded the victims with heavenly upliftment. Even God Himself made his presence known among the spirit rescuers and carers in the form of gentle waves of pulsating colour and effervescence, which imbued them all with inspired direction and guidance. Also, the Tsunami waves, however high and lethal in their force of destruction, carried still more unseen healing energy and radiance as they pounded onto the shores!

As we ourselves mingled among the thousands of other carers and comforters attending the various stages of the awakenings and disturbances of the earthly casualties, we were continually aware of the warmth of love emanating from the surrounding atmosphere of the special Recovery Realm. As a qualified doctor myself, called upon to research every patient I personally encompassed, I was deeply moved by the overwhelming peace pervading the hearts of all the other professionals in the field of medical and psychological understanding towards their own groups of casualties, as well as the nurses, counsellors and orderlies etc. It was as if every helper, whatever the category, every convalescent ward and private suite, every therapeutic hall and counselling room were imbued with loving affection and tranquillity from the continuous infiltration of soft healing energy, which was of such paramount importance.

Dear families and friends of all the beloved souls lost from Earth now received into Heaven, may I extend our very deepest sympathy and condolences from the Realms of Light. The separations between you all grieve us too beyond any words we can express, and the unseen healing radiance will surround each and every one of you day after day in your physical lives for as long as it is needed to uplift your own spirits, until you feel calmer, stronger and able to move forward more purposefully in your earthly destinies.

Your dear loved ones will also play their own part to support and comfort you, as already described, and you in your turn can send out thoughts to them, just as you would have spoken to them on Earth. It will help them feel that you too are aware they are 'alive and well', and can penetrate the ethers with your own 'bridge of love'. In God's own time, you may be rewarded with little signs that they have 'heard' and return their hearts of love to you. Best of all, you may meet them in your dreams as short unexpected encounters. This will all be part of your own recovery process, and may well lead you to a new awareness of the so-called invisible realties beyond death.

Once our own patients begin to fully recover from the traumatic change of consciousness, the heavenly radiance begins to rise within their new spirit souls. Their smiles light up the rooms, the gardens, and the surrounding landscape or town thoroughfares. Their anticipation of new studies, new pastimes, new careers, new vacations, new pleasures, new environments, brings cheerful countenances and a light spring to their steps.

All the new acquaintances made during the recovery, whether past relatives or new friends, plus the first visits to the earthly vibrations to see you, their true loved ones, imbues them with more inner radiance. It is by no means unusual for newcomers in Heaven to express their new joy of further existence by creating gifts in thought for their loved ones left behind in physical life, making advance plans to make them happy on birthdays, celebrations and anniversaries, and above all collecting mementoes, etheric videos, portraiture, poetry and flowers for the ultimate reunion one day, which for you may be many years, but for them it may seem only a few moments in eternity as they travel backwards and forwards in time. *(4.30pm)*

13.7.05 - 10.05pm

Many of you may be wondering, following my description of the long influx of radiance from Heaven beforehand, that we must have known long in advance of the pending natural disaster. We did indeed, very sadly! There was nothing we could do to prevent the terrible catastrophe, and I cannot describe the intense anticipation which was suffered widely in our dimensions knowing the likely enormous loss of life from Earth. The Rescue Realm was prepared in every possible detail, and the rescue training undertaken in deepest endeavour. I myself worked upon many contingency plans alongside colleagues and associates for some considerable time beforehand.

Future prediction for earthly calamities is carried out by our own very advanced so-called 'computer systems'. The reported information, timing and conclusions are always very exact allowing us due time to make our detailed plans for the rescue operations, and subsequent recoveries following the aftermath. In the case of man-made disasters, we try our utmost to avert the pending disasters through infiltration of warnings, and endeavouring to change the circumstances. We have many successes unknown to you, since many do not happen, but tragically others are often beyond repair and the inevitability of the disaster must be faced by us head-on! I assure you all, our darkest moments are standing by before the onslaught, knowing full well in advance the likely death toll, and the untold misery it will all generate on Earth and in Heaven.

We may not be able to save any disaster entirely, but we can often reduce the casualties to a minimum as far as possible. At every stage of all the rescue and recovery operations our hearts, minds and compassion are with you and your lost loved ones continuously, until all is well once more.

Let us return now to the 'End of the Rainbow'. What, you may now ask, is the Pot of Gold? This will vary according to the individual soul. What is true Heaven for one may be very different for another. Like a gold digger looking for treasure it may take time to find, but once found in true reward it will be secured forever.

Perhaps the dear Princess Diana finding her true vocation in Heaven is a classic example to illustrate our truth. She was tossed and torn in her emotional life on Earth, despite her many beautiful moments carrying out her duties in public with all the adulation she was given, but underneath was a sad heart. Ultimately, she was killed tragically amid a storm of national and world grief never before demonstrated so deeply for one person. But 'out of the ashes' a new Princess rose in her true virtues of dedication towards our children in need in Heaven. She not only found her Pot of Gold, it was placed quite naturally into her lap.

So you may now appreciate that all Pots of Gold are indeed very often the personal fulfilment of a deep yearning previously denied, and finally rewarded when the individual has proved their true worthiness of the privilege. However, you may not need to wait to come to Heaven before receiving your Pot of Gold. You may even find little Pots of Gold to enjoy from time to time in your physical life, and when you come to Heaven these may all add up to the one big Pot of Gold.

Only you, and you alone can determine how great your reward will be according to your deep need, and more importantly your sincere endeavours to make others happy despite your heartaches. All must balance out in strict worth of the privilege, so that the ultimate reward may be cherished forever. *(10.25pm)*
14.7.05 - 9.20pm

For those of you who knew your dear loved ones well on Earth, you may be able to build up a personal picture of their likely Pot of Gold towards which they may aspire in our higher dimensions. However, no true reward is given without painstaking diligence of purpose on the part of the recipient beforehand, plus a deep effort to give their true worth to the community. Deprivation can often bring the greatest appreciation of our prize or compensation, which is eventually received in ultimate joy and happiness.

Sincere love, romance and marriage continue to exist in the afterlife. This is perhaps an unexpected new concept for many of you on Earth. But I do assure you that true love is even deeper in Heaven's surroundings that reflect every joyful moment together.

Harmony of understanding, harmony of friendship, harmony of congeniality, and harmony of compatibility are sure ingredients of supreme happiness in married bliss. But like the Pots of Gold, this ultimate covenant must be tested and developed to its full potential beforehand. Permission will only be granted when each partnership fully qualifies every condition of love and harmony together.

Marriage partners in the highest Realms devote much time together in chosen vocations, working alongside each other, and also enjoying many outside interests in partnership. Social gatherings are full of every exchange of understanding, and small groups of devoted couples may work together in our communities. Every joy you experience on Earth is reflected in Heaven, but on a much higher wavelength of love and harmony attained through long development of spiritual values and practice.

Many of you on Earth are separated from your love partners in widowhood, which will become the true test of your hearts for the one you are separated from, whether in physical life or in Heaven. There is grief on both sides, as we have previously explained. The marriage reunion for those who come together again after long separation, and have no other partner meantime, is beyond description. They fuse once more in total ecstasy.

Others who are granted new partnerships on Earth in the interim period will also reunite in love with the original partner in companionship in our Realms, but a choice will ultimately be made as to which one was indeed the true love of all. This may take time, but it can also be quite instantaneous! If a man or woman is widowed more than once, the same rules will apply.

The only criterion for a true love partnership in Heaven is complete mutual adoration from the heart. Those passing into the afterlife must first wait for the development of new circumstances for the one left behind on Earth. Once more, their true love will be tested on both counts, and determine if they remain loyal to each other, or if each need to make a new start. Whatever the outcomes, past and future will come together in the final conclusions. Love, and true love alone will be the only binding chord forever.

Finally, those who have been denied a loving partnership at all due to difficult circumstances, family or community prejudice, or any other sacrifice, will be given very special opportunities in Heaven to develop their lost potential for this deep joy of being in love. *(10.33pm)*

17.7.05 - 12.10pm

Those who abuse their partners on Earth, physically or mentally, will be given appropriate periods of denial of any liaison until their hearts and minds begin to reconcile towards attitudes of a more loving approach. It has to be, to balance any cruelty they may have administered. God's true justice will always prevail, and this will also apply on Earth as well as in Heaven, as far as possible.

They must rise in great efforts and humility to redeem themselves. Every help and encouragement will be given to them every step of the way, until they truly understand that each individual soul is beholden to relate to another in love and deepest respect.

My dearest brothers and sisters of all nations and creeds in physical life, your earthly journeys are but the beginnings of greater journeys and pilgrimages in Heaven. Every experience you gain on Earth will prepare you, not only in the awareness of the true values and virtues of God's ordinance, but also in deeper understanding of the joys, and in contrast, the hardships of all human and other creature lives.

One day, you may be requested to enlist whatever experienced help you can offer to our devoted rescue teams in Heaven, which will demand every expertise available, and you will be honoured accordingly. No good work on Earth or in Heaven, however unseen, will go unnoticed by God, whose deep thanks and appreciation, however great or small will be given unconditionally in whatever way is appropriate to the individual concerned.

May I leave you now with a brief look at the various Spheres leading up from the Summerlands (the third Reception Sphere, which is beyond the first two Borderland Reception Spheres) to the Highest Realms of Light. Your journey in reality would take considerable time, since you must develop every spiritual virtue to raise the strength of your individual soul light and community awareness.

Those who show special promise in the Summerlands will be given the opportunity to visit the fourth Sphere of Aspiration, where souls learn the deeper more unified meanings of life. For instance, separate religions as you know them on Earth come together in greater understanding and respect of each other, and the central core of ethics common to them all prevails. Bigotry and prejudice is broken down. Community welfare is also given greater sense of care and responsibility among all cultures.

The next rung of the ladder towards highest Heaven is the fifth Sphere of Education. This amazing collection of Realms are devoted to the highest studies within their colleges and universities for the very cream of endeavour in every subject known to human kind. Diligent research is also carried out for future projects and inspiration for Earth, but far more advanced than any of you can envisage in your world. Past composers, past painters, past writers, past scientists etc of famous, and less famous repute, offer their own curriculums of experienced learning to chosen students, who have achieved appropriate standards to qualify for a special place in the academy concerned. This is not to say that education is not available in the lower Spheres. Every possibility is available in their Halls and Colleges of Learning, but they are the first and intermediate stepping stones to the advanced courses in the Sphere of Education.

Beyond those Realms is the sixth Sphere of Guides, each district containing the older cultures and civilisations as well as ancient native races, such as the Native Americans or Aborigines, who have all brought their own special contribution of philosophy to your civilised world. Many more recent cultures have now been added, to promote a very comprehensive collection of human spirit guides of every nation and creed, whose wisdom is taught to those seeking to take on this very worthy, but oft times thankless task of shadowing men and women on Earth throughout their physical lives, like an 'unseen' godparent. Many of the devoted souls in these Realms travel down the Spheres, to bring their mind infiltration development courses to those enrolling for this very necessary work of guidance and inspiration. They are truly God's messengers of wisdom.

Finally, we reach the seventh Sphere of Light, which I have already briefly described. I will only add that it is a beauty of existence beyond all imagination, and a happiness that supersedes all past fulfilments. I speak from my own personal experience. The Realms of Light also house the highest government and administration centres of ultimate love and responsibility. They are all palaces of great beauty and peace ruling not only the Sphere of Light, but also reaching down to influence each successive Sphere below, where lower government palaces preside in conjunction with the highest authorities above.

Governors serve long periods of office in true unity, love and peace within their dynasties, but at the same time linking in true co-operation with the residents of their communities, and with the other regional palaces. Supreme depth of understanding, supreme responsibility, and supreme peace in law and order are their sincere mottos.

This may all sound a far cry from Earth, and indeed appear an unimaginable utopia beyond reality in your terms. May I remind you all that the Realms of Light have been created over many millennia of painstaking aspiration towards the highest spiritual and human values of supreme understanding. A more modest achievement towards our example is well within your reach on Earth, and should be considered very seriously.

You cannot go on as you are amid turmoil and adversity without taking full stock of your deep responsibility and commitment towards world peace, world co-operation, world unity and above all love and respect for every nation and individual. We will guide you every step of the way, if you will put in your own true and sincere efforts towards the dream.

Your world 'Pot of Gold' awaits round the corner, when you have completed your painstaking labours and aspirations to that end, and your joy will be our ultimate joy as the Light of Heaven begins to descend to Earth at the 'End of Your Rainbow'.

My deepest peace and love be with you all."

(1.40pm)

Epilogue

HEART TO HEART by the Channeller

How do I follow that? I can only humbly offer my own thoughts upon this documentary and try to imagine your thoughts and feelings, especially if you have lost a loved one or loved ones through the terrible catastrophe. Together we may find a few more pieces to add to the jigsaw towards an even fuller picture. Perhaps we can come down to earth a little too, and try to see where we can move forward in this greater understanding. We will also take a look at the mechanics behind general communication from Spirit, discuss aspects of Heaven, and give you a short sketch of my own background.

TUNING-IN TO ANOTHER WORLD

Transcribing this special documentary from the Spirit or Heaven world has been for me, personally, a very moving and illuminating journey over the months it took to complete. I never know what is coming next with each instalment. Sometimes, I am given the odd preview, either just before or during transmission, to move my mind and telepathy forward for the writing, but even then it doesn't quite turn out as I expect. It's very like taking down a serial, so I'm always anxious to know what is coming next. As a clairaudient, I hear the spirit voices in my mind and take the words down like dictation.

Just before I begin, I say a prayer for guidance, ask for Heaven's radiance and love to fill the room where I sit, and the gift of psychic transmission to take it down as perfectly as possible for the benefit of higher knowledge and awareness on Earth. In between sessions, I leave it a day or so for the energies to build up again.

I am only the 'instrument' or 'secretary' taking down the clairaudient inspiration from the spirit voices. The words are not my words, and I cannot accept any credit for them whatsoever. As I write each part and section I learn volumes myself. There are always surprises on the way, and aspects of Spirit or the afterlife I hadn't previously considered. Every other Spirit disaster recovery sequence I have transcribed, has been very different from the previous one, either in the type of disaster with its individual rescue operation, the area of the world and situation, or the way it is put over from the inspirers.

Each one serves as a particular example for many other similar types of tragedy, such as earthquakes, sea disasters, aircraft crashes, explosions, massacres and so on. In this particular one, the unseen help is for the thousands drowning in the Tsunami waves and flooding inland. One minute the victims are on Earth, the next they are dramatically lifted into another consciousness. Tragically this is a common theme of most of the world's disasters, causing shock and horror on Earth.

I assure you, I never chose to do this work and specialised field of spirit communication. I was a good five years into the inspired writing before the pull to offer my services in this direction moved me into this area. At the time I was decorating a new home, standing on a ladder and attempting to paint my lounge walls on a day off from work. The television was on in the background to keep me company.

Suddenly, the midday news came on announcing the unexpected explosion of an American space capsule in mid air after its launching! Appalled at the tragedy, I stopped in my tracks to watch the pictures, and then carried on painting a little more deep in thought.

Minutes later, I reached out in my mind to Spirit asking whether I could help in any way to bring information through from their dimensions about those who had died in the capsule and how they had passed over? I ended up transcribing about four typed pages on the terrible incident. Little did I ever imagine at the time that this was the forerunner to other disaster sequels in the future, over many years. The main aim was to bring through the information and knowledge of the unseen help in the hope of bringing some form of comfort to the bereaved.

It hasn't always been a comfortable process for me during the communication. The details have often reduced me to tears, while I have been taking down the words. I am also very much mentally in the scene as I write, and that can sometimes be harrowing. Often I put my pen down at the end of an instalment and my eyes well up for all those lost, and for their families grieving for them in their shock and perhaps anger at God for taking them away! I'm sure anyone else would feel the same while transcribing disaster sequels.

This documentary has been no exception. As I take down the information in the hope of bringing insight and comfort to the bereaved on Earth, I feel so near and yet so far. In my mind I am linking what is revealed to me of those who pass into the afterlife with the agony of the loved ones left behind on Earth. This is so hard to put into words. It is like Heaven and Earth coming together at the same time. The Spirit words and visions help me to appreciate the depth of suffering on both sides of the 'great divide', and my heart reaches out to them all. During the weeks and months of completing a disaster sequel, I live, breathe, and cry my way through to the end. Even the very happy endings have their pathos.

There have been times when I stop and say to myself, "Why am I doing this?" The only answer is that Spirit seeks to bring comfort and the reassurance of the continuance of life after death for all those who have tragically lost their loved ones from a disaster, and for the greater understanding of the world in general. The same recovery principles will apply to all the various catastrophes, as well as to every other type of fatal accident communally or individually. Unseen helpers are always on hand to uplift the confused new soul or souls into the higher consciousness, following sudden and unexpected death!

HOW WE 'PASS OVER' INTO SPIRIT

At this point, let us look at the transition of 'passing over' and how that change takes place. Many people are already aware that each human being has an energy field surrounding their physicality. It has been proven by the means of Kirlian photography, which uses a vibrational technique to form the pictures. Even the leaves of plants show up as radiating an outline of vitality around their edges. Flowers have amazingly large and beautiful auras for their size, hence the growing field of flower essence therapy and their vibrational healing properties.

These 'unseen' energy fields are sub-divided into what many people term as our subtle bodies, which, in total, comprise our aura and extend beyond our physical body by two to three feet or more. There are seven fine vibratonal counterparts in replica to our material form, each one attached to one of the seven main energy centres known as chakras. Many psychics can see auras clairvoyantly, and can detect the varying colours according to the emotional mood and evolvement of each individual. The first, third, fifth and seventh subtle bodies are fixed in form in graded vibrational frequency from low to high, while the in-between subtle bodies of the second, fourth and sixth are more fluid and changeable according to emotional moods and fluctuating attitudes. They merge together as the sum total of our spiritual anatomy. This beautiful subject is a whole study in itself.

This whole invisible 'double' of our being interpenetrates, interacts and intercommunicates with our physical body through an unseen umbilical chord, known in spiritual circles as the 'silver chord'. Our auric counterpart is what the Australian surfer referred to as our 'back-up' body. This is the part which ejects out of the physicality, and rises up during 'near death experiences' (NDE) of which so many cases have already been reported and analysed. However, in such incidences, the 'silver chord' does not break, as in true death, but returns the unseen sublte body back into the earthly form to allow the individual to recover, and to fulfil the rest of their life in our material world. The black tunnel with the light at the end, so often described in NDE's, is merely the etheric 'birth canal' into the next world of the afterlife.

The deep feelings of enfolding love and bliss experienced in 'out of body' ejections during NDE's is the preliminary healing radiance to ease the separation of passing over either temporarily, or in the case of real death.

So, in conclusion, this auric double, for want of a better term, is in essence our spirit or soul. We do not gain it upon death, but rather carry it around with us on Earth! It is only when the 'silver chord' is broken, or cut completely from our body at normal or sudden death, that the spirit or soul is released into the Heaven world, where it becomes focused upon its new environment. But, as you now know from this communicated documentary, this initial adjustment may take time and several awakenings according to the circumstances.

I do hope this basic knowledge will help you to understand how we can transform from our physical body at death to the spirit counterpart in Heaven, and provide a more logical explanation of why we cannot 'see' our loved ones in the afterlife, who are just as much 'alive' as we are in physical life. They feel just as 'solid' or 'real' in their own vibrational wavelength or spirit dimension, in a similar way to our own dream state during sleep.

It is our own invisible auric being that can sometimes sense their presence. That unseen part of us is on the same level as they are in Spirit, like soul speaking to soul. When we come to realise that each and every one of us is multi-dimensional in make-up, and not just skin, bones, muscle, organs, blood circulation and nervous system etc, we can perhaps begin to make more sense of the mystery of death. What we see of ourselves in the mirror is only the 'tip of the iceberg'.

In a sense, we all live a 'double life', the main one concentrated upon this very physical and material existence on Earth, which is as it should be, and the other unseen one blends into our consciousness very quietly and subtly in the background, but nevertheless, remains the vital life force of our inner spirit or soul, and is the power behind the wheels of our physicality bringing us never ending energy, mentally, emotionally and spiritually. Without it we would not be alive in this world, and it is completely indestructible to any force, accident or disaster on Earth. We now know that when our turn comes to pop over into the afterlife at physical death, we shall take our 'back up body' with us to begin another fuller existence in Heaven.

HEAVEN SEEMS SO MUCH LIKE EARTH!

Perhaps one of the aspects of the Spirit dimension that may have surprised many of you is the fact that it appears to be so much like Earth! This is because our world has so many preconceived ideas about Heaven, which have not been qualified by metaphysical analysis. The original 'harps and trumpets' vision of the Middle Ages and Renaissance paintings reached out to a less educated population, who were bound by the doctrines of a Christian religion, which itself appeared to have little idea of the true reality. However, there may have been many natural mediums on the outskirts of society, perhaps working as herbalists and soothsayers, who perhaps knew more from inspiration, but kept the secrets to themselves in a somewhat hostile religious environment.

The advent of Spiritualism through the table rappings of the Fox sisters in America in the 19th Century brought a huge wave of interest in the afterlife. Many mediums brought through evidential information of past individuals during séances, and certain scientists took up the call to investigate invisible phenomena. A very general picture of the Spirit world has slowly emerged over the last one hundred and fifty years, and collaborated by many separate mediums with no connection between each other.

This picture reveals that loved ones passing over into the Spirit domains do not change their earthly personalities, but are often 'seen' much younger than the mature age at which they died.

Halls of Learning have been described. Also homes with books and furniture, gardens, plants, flowers and landscapes far more beautiful than on Earth. The progressive levels or Realms have been detailed from the lowest to the highest.

Animals, birds and wildlife are included in the descriptions. Personal pets are cared for by relatives already in Spirit, or trained, devoted animal/bird keepers in beautiful sanctuaries, until they can be reunited with their earthly owners in the fullness of time.

The freedom of travelling by instant thought transference or floating above the landscape is testified. Reception areas of rest and recuperation close to the Earth plane have also been written about, where many newly passed souls are cared for and helped in their adjustment to the new dimension of consciousness.

Spirit's channelled documentary for this book has perhaps gone a step further by putting over this rescue and recovery operation in a fairly down-to-earth manner, which may have been purposefully designed for us all in our world to identify with more readily. It aims to speak our 'language'. But there are, of course, many hidden differences, but these numerous details would take another book, or books, to complete.

This special documentary serves only to pass on a very general over-view of the Spirit dimensions and their dedicated rescue teams. Those passing in such trauma from a huge catastrophe, such as this one, are shocked and confused enough when they awaken to their new consciousness, without having to deal with a totally new environment quite alien to the one left behind on Earth.

The Heaven world is sensitive to all these needs, and tries to make them all feel as comfortable as possible in familiar surroundings. The rescue sequence also helps them to feel an emergency service has lifted them out of their predicament during the worst moments, and so psychologically lull their minds into a sense of safe security.

In this whole research into the reality of the Spiritual Realms, we must bear in mind that we are dealing with a world based on thought, which can build up and manifest *anything* from familiar articles, large or small, to buildings, interiors and the landscape, plus activities and events. There seems to be no limitation of imaginative thought creativity, within good reason, by those experienced in its every field. Even on Earth everything we invent, make or improve, stems from original mental inspiration.

Therefore, human beings arriving there from Earth will be happy to re-develop everything they had known and loved in physical life, from their own needs to the general community and environment, and all this would have built up over the centuries long before us. Naturally, we have gone through many stages of historical development through the many cultures and eras, all of which would have found their place in the afterlife.

But even Heaven moves on and every good memory of the past is also preserved. In truth, from many years of communication with the Spirit world, I have come to appreciate that on the higher levels, especially, they are far in advance of us, even up to several hundred years! A good illustration is the heavenly aircraft described in Part 2. We appear quite primitive in comparison.

They must in essence be ahead of us in order to bring guidance and inspiration to the right minds on Earth. If we could only tune in more deeply to their wealth of knowledge and wisdom, we could by our own efforts and motivation move forward in leaps and bounds, not only in general living standards, science and technology, but in more balanced sociability, morals and universal spirituality. Heaven's example shines through this documentary, which I feel offers us encouraging inspiration, like so many other wonderful books on the market.

SPIRIT COMMUNICATION AND MY OWN PSYCHIC DEVELOPMENT

Mediumship is also based on telepathic thought wavelengths. A trained and developed sensitive has learnt to tune into the higher octaves of 'seeing' and 'hearing', and to decipher and translate the many vibrational frequencies. In other words, while transmitting information from Spirit to this Earth plane, they have expanded their consciousness to coincide with their etheric or subtle body senses, the higher subtle 'eyes' and 'ears' and intuition. All of which can take many years of practice and experience to become proficient. Clairvoyance is 'clear seeing', clairaudience is 'clear hearing', and clairsensience is 'clear feeling'.

Psychic art is a growing form of mediumship bringing through portraits of loved ones and guides from Spirit. Continuing music from past composers is another transmitted phenomenon through mediumship. The general term of 'channelling' is now used to cover a wide range of Spirit inspired information and higher knowledge from accepted Spirit Guides and cosmic beings. Inspired writing is by no means uncommon, and many psychics bring through poetry, as well as teaching from higher Realms. I feel personally, we are still very much at the beginning of an exciting journey into the unknown, but we must be careful to tread slowly and wisely.

Like many others, I have been very lucky to have been brought into the Spirit-inspired way of life. I began spiritual healing in my twenties, and continued for many, many years before becoming clairaudient overnight, now 25 years ago! I never had any ambitions towards mediumship, it just happened! The 25th June 1980 was the most incredible day of my life! While getting ready to go to my part-time job in a soft furnishing and dress fabric store in our local town, I suddenly heard two lovely voices introducing themselves to me!

I was combing my hair in front of the dressing table mirror. The house was empty. My first husband had caught his train to commute to work, and I had taken my three growing children to their schools. I was entirely on my own. And there I was completely taken aback, but not in any way frightened.

The peace and love that came over me listening to these heavenly voices quelled all my fears. They were so kind and understanding as they spoke into my mind, and I felt compelled to answer them with my own thoughts. And so began a telepathic conversation, which sadly I cannot remember, because, as I now know after many years, as the heightened consciousness during spirit conversation comes back to normal daily thinking the memory fades. Something that all mediums experience. All I can recall now was asking these new unseen friends questions about life, and who they were on my way to work!

Sister Marie, a past nun, and Brother Albert, a past doctor, introduced me to other voices every so often during the hours of my part time work, before I left to pick up my children from school. I shall never know how I managed to get through that day appearing reasonably normal as I measured out curtain materials etc, for customers coming into the furnishing department, while my mind was operating on a two way circuit! It was mind blowing, and unfortunately I was ignorant at the time about protecting myself and 'closing down' the psychic energies. No wonder I was so mentally exhausted when I arrived home.

But the excitement had been worth it, and the spirit friends had protected me, anyway, knowing I was so new to the experience. That evening, I took down my first short communications through the clairaudient dictation, and was totally fascinated with this new phenomenon.

The days, weeks, and months passed as my communications grew, and notebook after notebook was filled. Very slowly I intimated to close family and friends about my new occupation. Fortunately, they accepted without suggesting I had 'gone off my head!' Apart from my husband remarking, "I thought you seemed a little daydreamy," no-one criticized me in any way. They all seemed very pleased and interested, and didn't doubt my intentions.

However, I myself developed doubts and queries over the months and years. No matter how real and natural it all appeared, as I took down endless writings in my spare moments, the very fact of its unseen intangibility created many questions in my own mind about its credibility. And so I experienced many phases of doubt over the years, sometimes closing down for months at a time to rehabilitate myself and take a rest. Each time the communications re-awoke they were stronger than ever!

Over the years I developed different kinds of information about the Spirit world beyond death. In the early days I took down messages for family and friends from loved ones in the afterlife. These helped to provide evidence for me. I kept a psychic diary, dating and monitoring short communications about my personal life. When I looked back on them weeks or months later they would take on meaning like small, fulfilled predictions. Other writings described lovely scenes and dedicated activities in the Spirit Realms. Also, they described the personalities of certain guides and their higher understanding and wisdom.

As I took down the communications from the different voices, I noticed the many individual ways that each personality put over their information. I would build up a feeling of each of their characters. It was like going through a door into another world, literally. A world which was calm, loving and understanding.

Coming back into this world again after transmission was often uncomfortable. Sometimes I even cried with the sharp contrast of the vibrations. Down here felt slow, heavy and unfeeling in comparison.

However, I had now learnt to conclude any clairaudient writing session with a mental 'closing down' procedure, to bring my mind and consciousness down to earth again after the light-headed spiritual wavelengths. Then, by drinking water and having a little to eat completed the grounding process. My longest development was trying to adjust, and find the balance between living in two worlds. It was by no means easy, as I'm sure other sensitives will agree. Spirit communication can be very uplifting and addictive.

The introduction of the first disaster episode took my writing into another dimension. As I progressed to describe other Spirit rescue operations I came to appreciate that perhaps this was my main role for the inspired dictation. The early ones were fairly short documentaries compared with one or two later books, which were communicated in the form of a fictional story with characters and conversations. I began to enjoy transcribing these very much, because they came alive and felt very real like a novel. This book has ended up a mixture of a documentary and true life narrative combined.

The rescue work carried out by many experienced mediums on Earth to help discarnate souls, who may be temporarily earthbound, pass into the light of the Spirit Realms in co-operation with heavenly guides and angels, is a very valuable service. It is a "bridge of love" between the two dimensions, and all our healing prayers and loving thoughts towards any soul passing over into Spirit will bring them further peace and upliftment.

PERSONAL BEREAVEMENT OF LOSING A LOVED ONE

I have also had the deep experience of personal bereavement after losing loved ones, and know at first hand how hard it can be to accept and work through the emotional pain. Even though I was a believer in the afterlife with the background of Spirit communication, I was still just like any other human being feeling the deep emotion of each loss. We are all the same, but I did have the advantage of knowing my own loved ones were in another higher dimension in Spirit, and it did help to a certain extent to cushion the sorrow. I also learnt more about the transition from their personal communications, but even these were very moving to write down.

For those of you who have lost loved ones in this particular Tsunami catastrophe, or any other, it must be an even deeper heartache. As I said in my brief introduction at the beginning of the book, you all have my deepest sympathy and understanding. I'm sure your mental and emotional traumas have felt quite beyond endurance at times since the happening, and never seem to get easier.

I do hope this sequel of your loved ones survival in the

Heavenly Realms has brought some grain of comfort to you, and the knowledge that so many helping hands were there to guide them through the very sudden transition following their tragic deaths. Also, all the love and care given to them as they awoke to the new consciousness, and slowly worked through their own adjustments to the new environment of thought manifestation.

I hope the vision of where they are, and how they are likely to continue their new lives in Heaven will help you to face your own lives again in this world without them. They will always remain very close to you in thought and love, and you can continue to remember them in your own thoughts of love. They are literally only a thought away. This is the 'bridge' for you to cross, whenever you wish, in your minds and hearts. They will feel and hear your call, and try to answer it in whatever way they know you will understand. Perhaps you will find a hidden photograph, hear a love song on the radio, watch a programme on the TV which they enjoyed, or some other reminder that they are really watching over your shoulder. You may even get a calm, happy feeling for the day.

Placing a few flowers by a framed photo on their Birthday, Anniversary or at Christmas will create a loving link from your heart to theirs. And may I suggest that you continue to go to the places they loved. I speak from personal experience. The first time may be the hardest, and tears may be shed, but it will help the healing process to build up new memories alongside the old, as you go with sympathetic family members or friends to support you. I do so understand how you feel touching all the memories, but make them your signposts towards recovery.

As the communicator suggests in her section on 'Visiting Earth' towards the end of Part Seven, some of you may have experienced the unseen presence of your loved one at some point in the weeks or months following the tragic event. This is fairly common because in the early stages of bereavement your mind will have been concentrating hard upon the loved one lost, and this creates an etheric vortex of energy wavelengths to draw their presence to you, and it gives them an opportunity of feeling close to you too. If it happens, thank them in your mind and send your thoughts of love in return. Your own subtle auric fields have picked up the signal unconsciously, and transferred it to your physical mind.

Some of you may long to receive a personal communication from them in the form of clairaudience or clairvoyance, and may be very disappointed if it doesn't happen. You were the closest person to them and therefore it should follow that you should receive their telepathy first hand, rather than through a medium.

Unfortunately, it is not very often that an untrained person can attain communication from a loved one in Spirit, because the tuning system between the physical mind and the spirit telepathy has not been properly opened up. It is not that the lost loved one doesn't want to get in touch with you personally, only that the so-called 'technical mechanism' is not in true working order. Also, in times of shock and mental turmoil, the mind is not relaxed and balanced enough to receive Spirit communication, even for those under deep stress, who are experienced in the field.

However, I hope it may prompt some of you to get the proper training and development to accomplish your end. *Please* don't try to go it alone. You must get the right guidance with the do's and don'ts. It can be a slow process, and far better that way. The reward of patiently getting it right will be worth the effort. Meantime, go to as many clairvoyant demonstrations as you can to see professional mediums at work, or pay for private sittings with reputable psychics. This will all add to your growing experience of the phenomenon. (For further information, names, addresses, phone numbers and websites are listed in the short Appendix at the end of the book)

NEW CONCEPTS, RELIGION, GOD'S UNCONDITIONAL LOVE

For many of you these concepts of life after death revealed in the channelling of this book may be new and bewildering. I do understand. I have had the distinct advantage of living with them for many years. I have also had time to sort out as much as I can, not only from the inspired writing, but from books, magazines, talks and seminars, and discussed the general field of metaphysics with numerous friends and acquaintances. My own quest for the truth began in my twenties. I am now in my early sixties. However, for those of you at the beginning of the search, whatever your age, I do hope this special documentary has answered some of the questions, but there may be many others unanswered that remain mysteries.

In these cases, I can only suggest that you scour the bookshelves in the libraries and shops under the appropriate sections for the subjects you are most drawn towards in the whole panorama of mystical science, psychic phenomena and new age spiritual philosophies. Weigh it all up in your mind until it feels comfortable to live with, and find opportunities to discuss the topics with other like minded people. Many minds put together can be very stimulating and offer more food for thought.

There are plenty of people out there in our world, who can shed light on many of these allied subjects. None of us know all the answers. The more we try to learn in this field, the more we realise how little we understand. It goes on and on, but that is part of our general evolvement. We are all in the same boat on a very exciting journey into the unknown.

The Tsunami disaster caught victims from many races and creeds. I do appreciate that for some of you these revelations may not fit your particular religious outlook. I personally have no prejudices about how anyone chooses to worship their spiritual philosophy. I feel there are many 'roads to God', or whatever you choose to call Him/Her. The only true religion is 'Love', and in Heaven the simple maxim is 'Love and Service' throughout the different Realms and Spheres, where all cultures and religious backgrounds reside alongside each other in complete harmony and respect.

If we make a brief study of the different creeds on Earth we will find many common denominators among them all at the core of their doctrines and ethics. We then begin to see a golden thread underlying each one of cosmic truth. A greater unity of thought and understanding will pave the way towards a more peaceful, tolerant and loving world.

Whatever our religion, we are all part of the divine, in as much as each and every human individual holds a spark of God within their being. Therefore, what we suffer, God suffers too! So, when the Tsunami catastrophe hit the coastlines and islands of the Indian Ocean Zone, God had already set up the heavenly rescue operation to uplift the newly released souls passing into the Spirit Realms. God had also organised enormous contingencies of help to mop up the mess of the aftermath, and enlisted thousands of willing and qualified spirit souls to comfort the injured and bereaved on Earth unseen, as well as fully care for all those suddenly and traumatically transferred to the Spirit recovery areas and Reception Centres in Heaven, offering the greatest compassion and understanding.

When the latter were more recovered and settled in their new environment, God paved the way towards new life and happiness in the Spirit dimensions in full compensation for their tragic deaths. In short, God was with us and suffered every inch of the way before, during and after the terrible catastrophe, as indeed with every other trauma, accident or major disaster.

How often people cry out on Earth after any severe calamity saying: "Why did God allow it to happen?" God didn't! Apart from our gift of freewill, let us consider all the mistakes we make, such as neglecting safety precautions; not always checking and overhauling machinery, transport and doubtful buildings; generally ignoring warning signs; allowing political and religious hatred and prejudices to build up, until unrest, anger, rising crime, terrorism and even war explode, causing countless casualties; demolishing much of the natural landscape where nature had created her own safety protective zones (not to mention the wildlife): and finally allowing too many of our populations to inhabit areas of extreme danger where earthquakes, volcanoes, landslides, tornados and flooding are likely to hit with little warning, and in this particular case, the huge devastating Tsunami waves. We are by no means innocent, and more often than not suffer the consequences of our own actions.

Instead of angrily reproaching God, perhaps we should be asking ourselves: "How did we allow it to happen?" How is God expected to combat our continuous wilfulness and even foolhardiness? We should bear all these possibilities in mind when assessing and taking full stock of the consequences of any disaster, in which people of all walks of life and age are sacrificed by becoming the unfortunate casualties, who just happened to be in the wrong place at the wrong time.

TRAGEDY ON EARTH – A 'SILVER LINING' IN HEAVEN

While transcribing this documentary I have felt very sensitive to all those of you who have lost loved ones so tragically in this catastrophe, and how you were likely to react to the rescue operation and recovery aftermath in the Spiritual Realms. I became painfully aware that reading it through might well bring back emotionally the traumatic memory of it all. This concerns me very deeply. I wish so much I could take it away, but it might prove to be the final release of anger, heartache and despair. And when the Sun comes out again, as it surely will, you may be more able to accept the continued existence of your dear loved ones in Heaven in greater comfort and calm, and feel more certain in your mind that you will one day be reunited with them in great joy. Where there is love there is no separation, ever. Even now you are still with them in your heart, and they with you in theirs.

Meantime, the more the unseen 'bridge of love' opens up

the 'divide' between Heaven and Earth, the closer the two worlds will become in the future. Life moves forward in mysterious ways. Perhaps the barriers that are broken down very dramatically on a humanitarian level after any disaster, may also have their equivalent between the Spirit world and our Earth plane. The trauma and loss of lives may motivate many people to look more deeply into the existance of the 'unseen' dimensions, opening up their minds to a new awareness and understanding of the afterlife.

In the coming years, if a new era opens up of special unity between our physical life and the Spiritual Realms, bringing them closer together as one, men and women may look back in that future to perceive a greater plan and outworking to compensate for all those sacrificed in this terrible catastrophe, and indeed many others before and after. In the fullness of time, Heaven may bring about the 'Silver Lining', and all those lost in the many deep tragedies will have contributed to this miracle, and you and they have been part of this awakening.

I assure you God will make it up to you all in every possible way down here for you, and 'up there' for your loved ones. Princess Diana's testimony in the story of her own heartbreak, and now her new happy dedication, is perhaps a living illustration to that end. Her own description of her passing at death, her awakening in the afterlife, and her subsequent early beginnings in Heaven, came as a complete surprise to me! I had been forewarned that she would feature in the part 'Attending to the Mass of Children', which made complete sense, but as I commented at the beginning of this epilogue, this became a classic case of it not quite working out as I expected.

When I sat ready to begin that section, a male voice came through introducing himself as a paediatrician, and I was completely flummoxed! I had to 'go with the flow' and of course it all opened out and I began to understand why, but it was only at the point of his introduction for her entry in communication that I became aware that her contribution was to be far more than about the help for the lost children from the Tsunami.

As she began to describe her passing, I was strongly aware of the emotional pain it was causing her in the process. It was a very moving section to transcribe, her passing, her awakening, her sorrow, her funeral and her deep gratitude for all the flowers in her memory. However, I do hope her new-found heavenly vocation brings comfort, joy and a healing balm to her close family members and friends, should this book come their way, as well as to our nation and the world in general.

So much has been written about her in books, and discussed in the media ever since her traumatic passing. Her loving memory will continue in many hearts all over the world. She endeared herself to millions of people across the nations. A stunning woman, who became an icon of human causes and suffering, but at the end of the day suffered her own very tragic and early death!

Let us salute her for being a brave ambassadress for the human causes so close to her heart, extending a compassionate arm to so many in need (often in private), and creating a spotlight of public awareness towards these problems. Her true gift to us was to open our hearts to so much that needed healing in our world. And now we know she continues her devotion and care in Heaven more deeply than ever.

As a mother, Princess Diana was the very best possible. She lived for her two lovely sons Prince William and Prince Harry. For their sakes, as well as her close family, let us keep the good memories alive and in peace. They lost her loving influence in their tender teens, a vulnerable age, but have coped amazingly well under the glare of the surrounding publicity. It could not have been easy, even with the help and support of those around them.

If this book should ever cross their paths, I do hope it may bring them special comfort to know she is 'alive and well', albeit in another dimension of existence, and that she continues to love and cherish their happy times together on Earth. Their knowledge of this will uplift and help her feel closer to them both, and perhaps they in turn feel closer to her in their own separations. At best, it may motivate the Princes to move forward in their lives in greater zest knowing her unseen blessing is forever with them. Peace and happiness be with them both.

The other casualties from the Paris car crash were Dodi Fayed and Jean Paul, whose bereaved families in physical life are still striving to salvage the truth about the terrible accident. If this book should come their way, I do hope it will bring them comfort and upliftment too. My task has been simply to transcribe the sequel in the afterlife, and therefore I cannot offer any light, as a psychic, upon the surrounding mysteries of the case. This is not my particular domain. The authorities on this level must be the ones to perhaps co-operate and help them all they can. I do hope it is all resolved satisfactorily.

Dodi's father, Al Fayed, has every reason to be happy that his son remains in close friendship with Diana in Spirit, and that he has found a new purpose and happiness in Heaven. Peace be with Al Fayed knowing his son is 'alive and well' despite the awful tragedy, as Dodi's life continues in another consciousness like that of the driver Jean Paul. Both send love to their families.

Our full attention of this book should remain focused upon the important theme of the Tsunami rescue work. I am sure Diana herself would agree, and that the inclusion of her own description of her sudden passing and resulting grief of being separated from her close loved ones on Earth, served only as a vivid illustration echoing the same countless similar feelings of separation among the Tsunami casualties in Spirit. Also her own devoted care towards the children simply mirrored the dedication of thousands of other carers working alongside her in the special Rescue Realm.

NEVERENDING COMPASSION AND LOVE 'UNSEEN' FROM ABOVE

While I was transcribing this special documentary the London bombings hit the headlines. More trauma, more tragedy, more losses! I mention this to explain that all the same principles of Heaven's recovery will apply to this disaster as well. The difference in this particular case would be that fire fighters would have come to the rescue from Spirit, instead of surfers. The victims would have felt strong hands pulling them out of the blaze, and taking them to safety into a very luxurious Reception Convalescent Centre not far from a beautiful lake. There they would have been given every comfort and help to recover from their sudden and unexpected transition.

I understand their recovery centre was in the extensive parkland of the Summerland Palace set in Oxfordshire style countryside, and their special upliftment gift, when they had fully adjusted to the new environment, was to be invited to a special garden party at the Palace and enjoy the amenities of the lovely gardens. I do hope this will bring comfort to the grieving families.

Since then one, two and three hurricanes have swept over New Orleans, Texas, Mexico and on to Florida leaving behind their devastating aftermaths. Once again the heavenly rescue teams have been on hand to comfort the victims passing into the afterlife, and support the emergency services on Earth for our survivors. The same would also apply to the countless casualties of the recent Pakistan and Indian earthquakes.

With all our continuing disasters, the higher dimensions have their heavenly emergency rescue schedules fully booked, with little respite in between the traumas. May we offer them enormous thanks and gratitude for their continuing help, love and compassion to our loved ones lost from Earth. We have little idea of the enormous wealth of unseen protection given to us all from the Spiritual Realms.

Well, I feel that just about sums it all up for the moment. I have meandered on for long enough. As for myself, I live a reasonably quiet life alongside family and friends in Southern England. Due to a serious illness three and a half years ago, my original strength and stamina has been reduced, and therefore I must pace myself accordingly. I have to be moderate in all my activities, and not travel too far. I hope to continue the inspired writing in peace and privacy, and hopefully find further opportunities to publish and share previous writings and channelled books, that have not had the chance to go forward in the past. I did try at the time, but it didn't work out. Spiritual awareness has grown considerably in more recent years, so perhaps there is more chance now of their acceptance.

It is now late evening and the night beckons me to bed as I write these last words…I am being interrupted from Spirit. Excuse me a moment while I investigate their message… *(9.55pm)*. How lovely. The heavenly 'Interflora' has just arrived!…I am 'seeing' the most amazing delivery of thousands upon thousands of bouquets, flower arrangements and baskets, pot plants, rose bushes, flowering shrubs, and hanging baskets. All your loved ones are sending them to you from the Tsunami Rescue Realm in token of their communicating reunion with you through this documentary.

Each card reads:-

"Dearest ………………….,
I/we still love you so much, and miss you. Be happy knowing I/we are well cared for in Heaven. Keep in touch by thought.
Fondest love always from,

………………………………

Well, perhaps some kind relative and friend could oblige on this level and send the physical equivalent to each one of you bereaved, to co-operate with Spirit and to fill in the appropriate names on the card message. It's called, 'Heaven and Earth working together'. And please do the same for other bereaved families who have also lost loved ones from other disasters. You may even be inspired to add something that would relate to both/all parties concerned as a very special anecdote of love and understanding, that you know would make the message deeply personal and meaningful.

I'll leave you now with these very loving thoughts. May Heaven's radiance heal your hearts in due course, may your lives open up to new opportunities and happiness, and may the world in general open its doors to Heaven's true existence.

My warm personal greetings to you all,

Sigrid

Photo Gallery of Loved One/Ones Lost in any Disaster

(Please palce your chosen photo or photos here)

DEATH IS NOTHING AT ALL

Death is nothing at all; I have only slipped away into the next room, I am I and you are you; whatever we were to each other that we are still.

Call me by my old familiar name; speak to me in the easy way which you always used.

Put no difference in your tone; wear no forced air of solemnity or sorrow.

Laugh as we always laughed at the little jokes we enjoyed together. Play, smile, think of me, pray for me.

Let my name be ever the household word it always was. Let it be spoken without effort, without the ghost of a shadow on it.

Life means all that it ever meant. It is the same as it ever was; there is absolute unbroken continuity.

What is this death but a negligible accident? Why should I be out of mind because I am out of sight?

I am but waiting for you, for an interval, somewhere very near just around the corner. All is well.

Canon Henry Scott Holland

PRAYER FOR PEACE

Lord make me an instrument of your peace

Where there is hatred, let me sow love;

Where there is injury, pardon;

Where there is despair, hope;

Where there is darkness, light;

Where there is sadness, joy.

O Divine Master, grant that I may seek not so much to be consoled as to console; to be understood as to understand; to be loved as to love; for it is in giving that we receive; it is in pardoning that we are pardoned, and it is in dying that we are born to Eternal Life. Amen.

Prayer of St. Francis

(Although these words are from a Christian Saint, I feel they are nevertheless Divine principles of human wisdom and spiritual aspiration to follow for all races and creeds on Earth).

SHINE BRIGHTLY, CHILDREN OF LIGHT

Holy ones. Take heart. The Earth and its people are in great need of you. Now, more than ever. It is time to speak up, to become visible, to share your wisdom with the world. No more hiding behind your façade of being an ordinary person. Time now to come out of the spiritual closet.

Have courage and do not fear. Rejection, persecution, humiliation are your fears. You have been ostracised before in this and other lives. People may shun you, laugh at you, turn their backs upon you. But you made a holy covenant with your Creator a long time ago. It is your purpose upon this planet. Did the Christ run and hide or did he declare his purpose? Did the Buddha? What of Ghandi, Martin Luther, Joseph Smith, Mother Teresa? Had they lived ordinary lives the world would have learned nothing.

In the darkness your light must shine. It must be bright and clear and visible. It is of no use to anyone if they cannot see it. The darkness in the world is blacker now than ever before. If a million lights were visible it would not be so dark. A million starts with one. It starts with you. Yes you. You know to whom I speak. Do not keep saying "One day I will…"

That day is now. God's warriors cannot let fear, shyness, or excuses get in the way of his service. This is your wake up call. Make a difference, now, today. No more excuses. Be as a light unto the darkness. With you are Angels and Great Masters eager to help you. They bring you courage, love and strength. Take their hands and together you can create a brighter tomorrow. Shine forth workers of light. Your value is without measure; our love without end.

Channelled by © Alison White - 9th June 2004
Source: Buddha figure

A BLESSING FROM THE BIRDS

Sweet Spirit, may the power of Eagle give you strength and guidance in this life.

May the wisdom of Owl guide and direct you and teach you the beauty of the night.

May the keen sight of Hawk give you clarity and insight.

May the magic and humour of Crow help you to laugh and dance along the way.

May the peaceful beauty of dove soften the winds of fate in your personal universe.

May the grace of Swan permeate your consciousness and give you balance.

May the voice of Jay teach you to speak your truth clearly.

May the brilliance of Cardinal warm your heart and bring you love.

May the dignity of Crane teach you the value of integrity and faithfulness and sustain you when life's lessons are challenging.

May the giveaway of Turkey gift you with a generous heart.

And may the flight of Heron lift your spirit and keep your purpose clear and bright.

May the broad wings of Condor shelter you from storms.

And may the healing powers of Vulture keep you clean and strong.

May the flight of goose keep you directed and secure on your path.

And may the iridescent beauty of Hummingbird fill your life with rainbows and lovely reflections of all that is.

May the grace of Egret fly you through your dreams.

And may the playfulness and intelligence of Parrot remind you to play like a child, with joy.

And may Bluebird always sing you the song of happiness.

(Author unknown)

APPENDIX
Useful Names and Addresses

The following names and addresses are not part of the earlier book, but have been kindly offered by the organisations concerned for any reader seeking further information and help.

1. NATIONAL FEDERATION OF SPIRITUAL HEALERS (NFSH)
Old Manor Farm Studio, Church Street, Sunbury on Thames, Middlesex, TW16 6RG

Telephone: 01932 783164

www.nfsh.org.uk

2. THE SPIRITUALIST ASSOCIATION OF GREAT BRITAIN (SAGB)
33 Belgrave Square, London, SW1X 8QB

Telephone: 020 7235 3351

www.sagb.org.uk

3. THE GREATER WORLD SPIRITUAL CENTRE
3-5 Conway Street, Fitzrovia, London W1T 6BJ

Telephone: 020 7436 7555

www.greaterworld.com

To spread in all directions the truth of survival after death, of spirit communion, of healing by the power of the Holy Spirit and to disseminate the teachings received from highly evolved spirit messengers.

4. THE COLLEGE OF PSYCHIC STUDIES
16 Queensberry Place, London SW7 2EB

Telephone: 020 7589 3292

www.psychic-studies.org.uk

5. THE SPIRITUALISTS NATIONAL UNION
Redwoods, Stansted Hall, Stansted Mountfittchett, Essex, CM24 8UD

Telephone: 0845 4580 768

www.snu.org.uk

6. PSYCHIC NEWS

The Coach House, Stanstead Hall, Stanstead Mount Fittchett, Essex CM24 8UD

Telephone: 01279 817050
Fax: 01279 817051
Email: pnadv@snu.org.uk

7. ARTHUR FINDLAY COLLEGE (Psychical Studies)

Stansted Hall, Stansted, Essex, CM24 8UD

Telephone: 01279 813636
www.arthurfindlaycollege.org

8. THE SCOTTISH SPIRITUAL COLLEGE AND HOLISTIC HEALERS ASSOCIATION

79-81 Bowman Street, Glasgow, G42 8LF

Telephone: 0141 423 5952
www.scot-spirit-col.co.uk

Non-sectarian eaching College and Association reaching across the board to all who wish to progress in their spiritual work.

9. THE WHITE EAGLE LODGE

New Lands, Brewells Lane, Liss, Hants, GU33 7HY

Telephone: 01730 893300
www.whiteagle.org
www.whiteaglepublishing.org.uk
www.thestarlink.net

Spiritual teaching and unfoldment, meditation, healing, retreats and bookshop.

Through White Eagle's teaching we are encouraged on a path of love, tolerance and service towards all life; towards the development of inner peace, and the awareness of our eternal spiritual nature.

10. STAR ACTION (Registered Charity No. 11111137)

Flat 2, 44 Kensington Park Gardens, London W11 2QT

Star Action has a number of projects in the Tsunami devastated parts of easter Sri Lanka, including the Tamil Tiger controlled zone from which larger charities have generally withdrawn their staff on safety grounds.

11. ALISTAIR HARDY SOCIETY

Supporting The Religious Experience Research Centre (RERC)
University of Wales, Lampeter, Ceredigion,
SA48 7ED
Telephone: 01570 424821
www.alistairhardyreligiousexperience.co.uk

The Alistair Hardy Religious Experience Research Centre and Society seeks through research and study to contribute to the understanding of transcendant, spiritual or religious experiences and their role in the evolution of consciousness and religious reflection, as well as their impact upon individual lives and on society.

12. FOUNTAIN INTERNATIONAL

P.O. Box 52, Torquay, Devon, TQ2 8PE
Telephone: 01371 831704
www.fountain-international.org

For the promotion of the natural healing of people and communities through the use of Spritiual and Earth energies. Free CD 'Helping to Heal the World'.

13. CYGNUS (BOOKS)

Freepost SS1193, Llangadog, SA19 9ZZ (UK)
CYGNUS (BOOKS)
P.O. Box 15, Llandelio, SA19 6YK, UK (from outside UK)
Telephone: 0845 456 1977 (UK)
or 01550 777 701 (UK)
+44 1550 777 701 (Outside UK)
www.cygnus-books.co.uk

Selecting the best Mind Body Spirit books from the 100s published every month, and made available at reduced prices in a monthly magazine "The Cygnus Review".